INSIGHT POCKET GUIDES

Sarawak

APA PUBLICATIONS

Part of the Langenscheidt Publishing Group

L

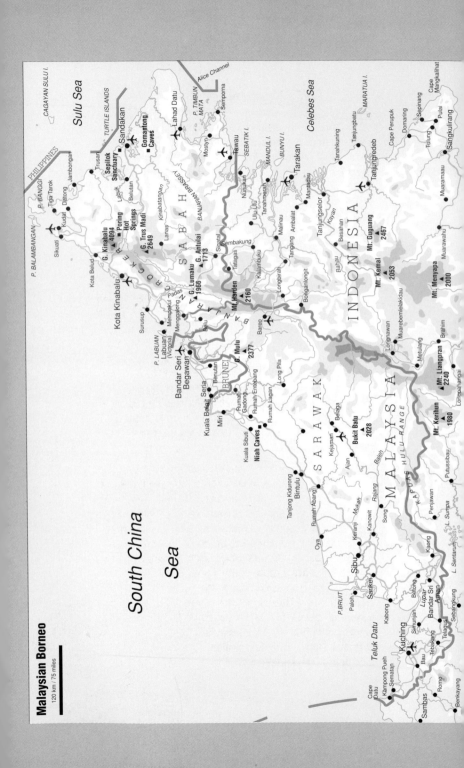

Malaysian Borneo

120 km / 75 miles

South China Sea

Sulu Sea

Celebes Sea

PHILIPPINES

CAGAYAN SULU I.

P. BANGGI

TURTLE ISLANDS

P. BALAMBANGAN

Sikuati
Kudat
Datong
Jambongan
Iga Tarok

Banggi

Trusan
Labuk
Belutan
Sandakan
Sepilok Sanctuary
Gomantong Caves
Lahad Datu
P. TIMBUN MATA

Alice Channel

Kota Belud

G. Kinabalu
4094
Poring Hot Springs
Kinabatangan
Lamag
G. Trus Madi
2649
Mostyn
Tawau
Semporna

Kota Kinabalu

C R O C K E R

Menggalong
Sipitang
Sembakung

S A B A H

B A N J A R A N

Nunukan
Ulu-Ulu
Tanahmerah
Tarakan
MANDUL I.
BUNYU I.
MARATUA I.

Surusup

Membakut
Padas
Belud

G. Lumaku
1966
G. Antulai
1713
Tatagas
Mantarihu

Cape Mangkalihat

P. LABUAN
Labuan
(Victoria)

B A N J A R A N

Mt. Harden
2160
Kalambuku
Tangang
Ambalat
Tanjungselor

Tulung
Pulai
Sangkulirang

Bandar Seri Begawan

G. Mulu
2377

Bareo

Longbirah
Bonganlongit
Kajan
Besahan

Tanjungredeb

Cape Perupuk
Domaring

BRUNEI

Benutan
Rumah Gadong
Rumah Enabang
Long Pila

Mt. Guguang
2467

Muarawahu

Kuala Belait
Seria

Rumah Lagan

Bahu

Muaramaau

Mt. Kemal
2053

Miri

Kuala Sibuti
Niah Caves

S A R A W A K

Baleh

I N D O N E S I A

Muarebemlelakidau

Mt. Menyapa
2000

Bukit Batu
2028

Kejaman
Belaga

Metulang

Brahim

Tanjong Kidurong

Bintulu

Rumah Abano

Ajan

H U L U   R A N G E

Longnawan

Mt. Liangpran
2240

Loinpaharigal

Oya
Mukah
Song
Rajang

M A L A Y S I A

Penjawan

Mt. Kerihun
1980

Kerani
Kanowit

Putussibau

Keraniji

Sibu
Sarikei

K A P U A S

Kaong

Paloh

Palau

P. BRUIT

Kabong

Betong
Lupar
L. Sumpa

L. Sentarum

Teluk Datu

Sematan
Kampong Pueh

Simunjan
Bandar Sri Aman
Sebangkung

Cape Datu

Bau
Kuching
Tebakang

Telagus

Roban

Benkayang

Sambas
Samba

Sulu Sea

Welcome!

Sarawak is the embodiment of Borneo, an untamed land of mighty rivers and rainforests filled with rare plants and animals. Here you will find some of the world's most dramatic caves; discover the era of White Rajahs in the capital of Kuching; experience traditional longhouse hospitality among folk who were once headhunters; explore old Chinese bazaars and visit timeless coastal villages.

In the following pages, Insight Guides' correspondent in Sarawak, Wendy Hutton, introduces you to her favourite areas of this huge state in a series of itineraries which are grouped around three main centres: Kuching and the southwest of Sarawak, where surprisingly accessible wildlife and the state's best beaches are found; central Sarawak around Sibu, including the mighty Rajang river, famed for its Iban longhouses; and Miri and the northeast, with the magnificent caves of Niah and Gunung Mulu, and the remote Kelabit highlands. She'll help you track down accommodation, find the best food and buy the local specialities, giving tips that only an insider would know.

Wendy Hutton, a writer and editor who has worked in Southeast Asia for 30 years, fell in love with Sarawak during her first visit to a remote Kayan longhouse in the 1970s. She has returned countless times, especially since setting up her base in neighbouring Sabah in the late 1980s. 'I never cease to be amazed at what Sarawak has to offer. No matter how many times I visit, there is always more to discover,' says Hutton. In this book she shares her favourite places with you in the hope that you, too, will fall under the spell of Sarawak.

C O N T E N T S

Pages 2/3:
Deep in the
rainforest

Pages 8/9:
Iban girls welcome
visitors

HISTORY & CULTURE

If Borneo didn't exist, some romantic 19th-century writer would probably have made it up. A vast island covered by rainforests bursting with unheard-of species of plants and animals. A land where pirates and headhunters, Muslim sultans and English rajahs, Chinese gold miners and nomadic tribes hunting with blow-pipes all went about their business.

Sarawak, a sprawl of green blurred at the edges by the South China Sea on the northwest of the world's third largest island, is Borneo personified. Cavemen lived here at Niah more than 20,000 years ago, fashioning simple flake tools, while other hunter-gatherers left remains of their meals of shellfish and animals in the cave of Gua Sirih near Kuching. But these early people completely disappeared from Borneo, to be later replaced by Austronesians who came by boat from the north in around 2500BC.

Glass and stone beads, earthenware pottery and iron tools give only fleeting glimpses of Sarawak's pre-history. A stone statue of the Hindu elephant god, Ganesh, and another of a Buddha seem to indicate that traders (probably from Sumatra) visited Sarawak's shores more than a thousand years ago. The Chinese made regular voyages south on their junks from AD900, exchanging porcelain for such exotic items as rhinoceros horn, sharks' fins, birds' nests and hornbill casques.

The Europeans arrived much later: the first detailed account of a visit to Borneo was provided by Magellan's chronicler, Pigafetta, in 1521. The riches of the East were an irresistible magnet for Western traders and adventurers, first the Portuguese, followed by the Spanish, Dutch, British and French. Over the next three centuries

Sarawak's virgin rainforest

they established trading posts and colonies from Goa on the west coast of India to Ternate in the Indonesian Spice Islands.

The Dutch, after several abortive attempts in the 18th century, finally managed to get a toehold on Borneo during the 1820s, signing treaties with the Muslim rulers in Sambas and Pontianak on the west coast and Banjarmasin to the south. Soon it was to be Sarawak's turn.

Stamford Raffles, the founder of modern Singapore, was, like many other colonial administrators, greatly interested in the trading potential of Borneo. Piracy was a serious problem, with local Dayak tribes, as well as bloodthirsty Illanun and Balanini raiders from the southern Philippines, attacking passing ships and settlements near the coast. Nonetheless, the possibility of profit continued to fire the imagination of merchant adventurers.

One such man, who had undoubtedly read Raffles' articles on Borneo's potential, was James Brooke. Born in 1803 in India, Brooke gave up his first career as an officer in the East India Company to try his hand at trading in the East on his own account. He also professed to be intent on substituting a 'just and benevolent administration' to free the natives from 'misrule and oppression'.

On his father's death in 1835, James spent most of his inheritance purchasing a schooner, the *Royalist*. Eventually, he arrived in Sarawak in 1839, where he met Rajah Muda Hashim, who was responsible for governing the region on behalf of his nephew, the Sultan of Brunei. Almost as if stage-managed to confirm the stories of piracy in Borneo, Brooke's party was attacked as he left Sarawak; however, the pirates were no match for the guns of the *Royalist* and Brooke returned safely to Singapore.

James Brooke

When Brooke came back to Kuching in 1840, Rajah Muda pleaded for his help in putting down a Dayak rebellion, promising to give him the land of Sarawak and Siniawan if he agreed. Brooke managed to negotiate a settlement with the insurgents, and eventually a document was drawn up in 1841 declaring him the 'Rajah and Governor of Sarawak' in exchange for a small annual sum payable to the Sultan of Brunei.

Thus began a century of rule by what one historian has described as 'benign despots', the so-called White Rajahs of Sarawak. James Brooke, who never married, made the eradication of piracy top of his agenda. He was greatly helped in this by the Royal Navy, which was interested in protecting the trade route between Singapore and Hong Kong. However, he managed to antagonise the Chinese gold miners working around Bau and lost his home and its contents during a rebellion in 1857. The profits which James Brooke had envisaged were not as lucrative as anticipated, and it wasn't until several years after his nephew, Charles Brooke, took over – James returned to England in 1865 – that the Sarawak government actually balanced its books for the first time.

The extent of James Brooke's Sarawak (which comes from *serawak*, the Malay word for the mineral antimony) ranged from the land west of Kuching to Tanjung Datu, and east as far as Samarahan (today almost a suburb of Kuching). The Brookes successively absorbed chunks of land previously controlled by Brunei until Sarawak achieved its present size in 1905.

Charles Brooke, while lacking the charisma of the first White Rajah, proved to be a solid administrator who was thoroughly devoted to eradicating headhunting and bringing peace and security to Sarawak. He was succeeded by his second son, who became known as Rajah Vyner Brooke, in 1917. The third White Rajah was an ineffective if benign ruler.

Turn-of-the-century transport

During the Brooke era, very few roads existed in Sarawak. Transport was by boat or on foot, and the various English residents given charge of isolated districts exercised considerable power. Some of them (particularly Charles Hose, who was in charge of the Baram district for many years) were keen amateur anthropologists and naturalists.

Charles Brooke was responsible for the establishment of the Sarawak Museum in 1891, and for attracting a series of noted travellers, naturalists and adventurers to the state. Christian missionaries and teachers, initially Anglican, followed by Methodists and Catholics, were encouraged, yet Charles Brooke was anxious to protect the upriver Iban and Orang Ulu tribes from what he saw as the depredations of coastal Muslims and supposedly wily Chinese traders.

The Past Half Century

In 1941, the centenary of Brooke rule, Rajah Vyner established the Council Negeri, ceding his absolute authority by giving the council the right to approve of all legislation and expenditure. The developing economy and infrastructure were shattered that year by the arrival of the Japanese, who occupied the state until 1945. It is widely accepted that during this period, headhunting – firmly suppressed under the Brooke regime – saw a resurgence.

When World War II ended, Vyner Brooke realised that he could not afford to restore Sarawak and, in 1946, announced his intention to cede it to the British as a Crown Colony. This proposal met with considerable resistance, especially among a group of Malays who supported Vyner's nephew, Anthony Brooke, in his ambition to become the fourth White Rajah. Nonetheless, in 1946 Sarawak became a Crown Colony.

Kuching Court House

Helped by the high prices for rubber and pepper — of which it is still an important producer — Sarawak entered a period of prosperity and development with the construction of roads, airports, hospitals and schools. But the drive for political change that swept Asia in the years after World War II was soon to involve Sarawak.

In 1961, the Malayan Prime Minister, Tunku Abdul Rahman, suggested the formation of a broader political entity comprising Malaya, Sarawak, North Borneo (now Sabah), Singapore and Brunei. There was considerable local sentiment in favour of a Borneo alliance of Sarawak, Sabah and Brunei, either as an alternative to, or a step towards, a wider federation. However, the various Brunei states were threatened by Indonesia's policy of *konfrontasi*, which was opposed to the formation of Malaysia, and by a rebellion against the Brunei sultan which erupted in 1962. A further complication arose when the Sultan of Sulu, in the southern Philippines, claimed that Sabah belonged to him.

Threatened on several fronts, both Sarawak and Sabah decided to join Malaya and Singapore to form Malaysia in 1963, negotiating special terms (known as the Twenty Points) that would give them some degree of autonomy. Brunei decided to keep its oil wealth and remain independent, and Singapore left the federation two years later.

Resistance to a greater degree of control from Kuala Lumpur than had been envisaged initially created tensions between the federal government and both Sarawak and Sabah, resulting in the replacement of their chief ministers by more 'co-operative' politicians.

A period of communist insurgency was to trouble Sarawak for a decade after the formation of Malaysia. Some of the 'communists' were, in fact, nationalists seeking an independent Sarawak. However, their cause was doomed and, despite causing considerable trouble from their hideouts (mostly along the border near Indonesian Kalimantan), the movement was eventually wiped out.

With its sizeable Muslim population (around 20 percent of the state's total of 3.8 million), Sarawak has maintained good relationships with the federal government. The first direct general elections held in Sarawak, in 1970, led to the installation of a coalition government comprising the Sarawak Alliance and the Sarawak United People's Party (SUPP), headed by Datuk Haji Abdul Rahman Ya'kub. He remained as Chief Minister until resigning in 1981, when he was replaced by Datuk Patinggi Taib Mahmud, who still held power in 1998. The coalition Barisan Nasional government still includes the SUPP, joined by the Sarawak National Party and the Parti Bumiputra Bersatu.

Just as Iban textiles are woven with different dyed threads, so the human fabric of Sarawak is composed of a complex mixture of ethnic groups and sub-groups. The word *dayak*, which means inland, was once used by outsiders to refer to Borneo's indigenous peoples; it was not used by Sarawak's people themselves until recently, when it seems to have become 'politically correct' (as it always has been in the Indonesian portion of Borneo, Kalimantan).

Forming almost 30 percent of the population, the Iban are the most numerous Dayak group and are renowned for their energy, extrovert personality and sense of humour. Originating in Kalimantan, the Iban migrated into what is now the Sri Aman district and up into the Rajang river basin. Somewhat confusingly, although the Iban lived upriver in communal longhouses, they were known during the Brooke era as Sea Dyaks, because they were often recruited as pirates. Once feared as Borneo's fiercest headhunters, the Iban — renowned for their fine *ikat* textiles — are now found in all walks of life, in the cities and in the modernised longhouses, where they grow pepper, rubber and other commercial crops as well as traditional hill rice.

Known previously as Land Dyaks, the Bidayuh are a gentle, tolerant folk who suffered countless attacks and slave raids by the Iban and Brunei Malays. Unusually, their longhouses were built inland rather than on the banks of a river. Today, the Bidayuh form a little under 9 percent of Sarawak's population, living in the west of the state towards Lundu and in the Samarahan division to the east of Kuching. Their basket ware, mats and etched bamboo work are highly regarded. Like the majority of Iban, most Bidayuh follow the Christian faith.

A large number of groups are referred to collectively as Orang Ulu or 'Upriver People'. Two of these, the related Kayan and Kenyah, had a stratified society with nobles, ordinary people and slaves, quite unlike the egalitarian Iban. Perhaps it was the existence of this leisured class that encouraged the Kayan and Kenyah to develop skills in creating the finest beadwork, woven mats and carvings. The Kayan and Kenyah crossed into Sarawak from the mountainous Apo Kayan in Kalimantan and settled in longhouses in the upper Rajang, Baleh and Baram regions. They are fairer skinned than many other ethnic groups and their music, costumes and crafts are quite different from those of the Iban.

The Kelabit and Lun Bawang, part of the Orang Ulu group, are found in the highlands around Bario and in the Lawas district, where they have developed a sophisticated irrigation system for growing rice. A number of enigmatic patterns carved on megaliths are still found in the

A Kenyah man

Kelabit highlands. Also classified as Orang Ulu are a number of very small groups, including the Punan, Punan Bah, Penan (of whom only around 600 still maintain a semi-nomadic lifestyle), Sekapan, Kejaman, Lahanan and Tanjong.

Believed to be one of the indigenous groups of Sarawak, the Melanau live mainly in the Rajang, Mukah and Bintulu regions. Many of them have converted to Islam, although the shamans who cure patients using carved figures (*belum* or *dakan*) are still found among the pagan and Christian Melanau. The Melanau harvest the sago palm around the Mukah region and are also fishermen.

Sarawak's Malays are a remarkably diverse group, unified by their Islamic faith and their custom of living in single-family dwellings rather than longhouses. They are a mixture of Borneo groups, including Brunei Malay, Melanau, Kedayan, Bidayuh and, more recently, Javanese. Traditionally coastal dwellers, the Malays prefer fishing to the cultivation of rice practised by most of Sarawak's other indigenous groups.

An ornate Chinese temple

Thousands of Chinese who had been prospecting for gold in Pontianak and Sambas in West Kalimantan began moving into Sarawak in the 1840s, particularly to the Bau district where gold, coal and antimony were mined and birds' nests were found in the limestone caves. Many Hokkien Chinese moved from Singapore to the Rajang district, although they were later swamped by Foochow Christians who still dominate the region of Sibu. Other Chinese migrated directly from China to work as farmers and traders. Initially prevented by the White Rajahs from staying overnight in upriver longhouses, some Chinese lived in and traded from their boats and, over the decades, many married local women. They were eventually given citizenship and now form about 28 percent of Sarawak's population.

A Buoyant Economy

Sarawak's economy is largely dependent on primary production. Although selective logging is practised, the rich rainforest is disappearing at a disturbing rate, in order to satisfy the world's demand for tropical hardwood. Large areas of land have been transformed into oil palm plantations and, to a lesser extent, planted with cocoa and rubber. Government land settlement schemes to encourage local landowners to lease their land for the creation of large oil palm plantations have met with limited success so far, as many are reluctant to give up their independent, traditional lifestyles and work on the estates controlled by a management company.

Sarawak is one of the world's major pepper producers, and although this crop was initially established by the Chinese, it is increasingly in the hands of the Iban and other indigenous groups. Other crops include coffee, tea, rice and copra.

Sarawak is blessed with oil deposits off its north coast, and although the state receives only 5 percent of the total revenue for this (petroleum rights belong to the Malaysian national oil company), a certain amount of employment is created on the oil rigs and in the refineries. A huge liquefied natural gas plant is located in Bintulu, which also has the world's largest granular urea plant, producing ammonia and urea for use in fertilisers and plastics. Although oil, natural gas and timber make up close to 90 percent of the state's exports in terms of value, manufacturing is increasingly important. New industrial estates created near north Kuching, joined by a new deep-water port and power station, all promise to help reduce the state's dependence on primary industry.

Longhouse Life in the Modern Era

Life in the longhouse, as in all other areas of Sarawak, has undergone tremendous changes in the past couple of decades. With many of the young men away working in logging camps or sawmills, on oil rigs or in the towns, and with those who have stayed planting cash crops rather than continuing a subsistence lifestyle, money and consumer goods have moved into the longhouses. It is increasingly rare to find old-style longhouses on stilts, as the government encourages cement floors and modern sanitation rather than the recycling once carried out by the longhouse pigs. Blackened skulls rarely hang from the rafters, and you won't see the men sitting around in loincloths; they're more likely to wear shorts as they watch TV powered by the longhouse generator.

Despite such changes, the harmonious, self-regulated communal life of Sarawak's longhouse dwellers goes on. The hospitality is as fantastic as ever, and ritual welcomes are still performed. Most longhouse folk are hard-working farmers, and many of the women also find time to weave fabric, baskets, mats and hats. They welcome visitors into their lives with unrivalled generosity and grace.

A family of longhouse dwellers

Historical Highlights

35,000–20,000BC A human skull excavated at Niah Cave provided evidence of human habitation in northern Sarawak during the Palaeolithic era.

AD700–1400 Archaeological remains indicate that trade existed between coastal settlements of northern Borneo and China, and with Hinduised Malays in Sumatra, during this period.

AD900 The Chinese begin making regular voyages south, exchanging porcelain for such exotic items as rhinoceros horn, sharks' fins and birds' nests.

1504–7 The first European believed to have reached Borneo was Italian Ludovico de Varthema.

1521 Pigafetta, chronicler for Magellan's fleet, recorded in detail their visit to Brunei.

1820s The Dutch colonial government, after several abortive attempts in the 18th century, gradually began to assert its influence over southern Borneo, signing treaties with the sultans of Pontianak, Sambas and Banjarmasin.

1840 An English adventurer, James Brooke, helped Rajah Muda put down a Dayak rebellion against the Sultan of Brunei in exchange for control over the countries of Sarawak and Siniawan.

1841 James Brooke officially became Rajah and Governor of Sarawak on 24 November.

1853 The borders of Sarawak pushed northeast to include most of present-day Sri Aman.

1857 In an abortive uprising, Chinese gold miners burned down the fort in Kuching.

1861 Sarawak's area more than doubled as James Brooke took over the entire Rajang basin and land as far north as Bintulu.

1865 Charles Brooke, James' nephew, unofficially took over as the second White Rajah when James retired to England.

1870 Charles Brooke was officially proclaimed Rajah of Sarawak two years after the death of his uncle.

1871 The town of Sarawak changed its name officially to Kuching.

1882 The River Baram region was added to the Brookes' domain.

1888 Sarawak was afforded the protection of the British Crown.

1905 With the inclusion of Lawas and Limbang areas over a 20-year period, Sarawak finally achieved its current borders.

1917 Charles Vyner Brooke, son of the second White Rajah, succeeded his father as head of Sarawak.

1924 An important peace ceremony was held at Kapit to end four decades of feuding between the Iban and other ethnic groups.

1941–5 Sarawak occupied by Japanese forces and most of the colonial administration interned at Lintang Camp.

1946 Rajah Vyner Brooke ceded control of Sarawak to the British and it became a Crown Colony, despite an uprising by anti-secessionists supporting Vyner's nephew, Anthony Brooke.

1948 District Councils were set up under Local Authority Ordinance. A period of prosperity began.

1963 Sarawak became independent with the formation of Malaysia, comprising Sarawak, neighbouring Sabah, the Federated Malay States and Singapore.

1970 Sarawak's first direct general elections held, resulting in a coalition government headed by Datuk Haji Abdul Rahman Ya'kub.

1981 With the resignation of Ya'kub, Tan Sri Abdul Taib Mahmud became Chief Minister, a post he still held in 1998.

Sarawak

60 km / 38 miles

South China Sea

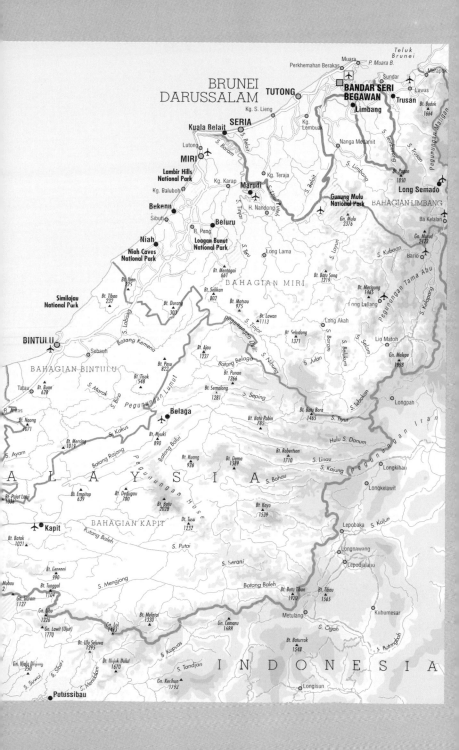

Kuching & The Southwest

Sarawak's capital, Kuching, one of the most charming cities in Southeast Asia, is surrounded by a wide variety of attractions. The following seven itineraries introduce you to the best of Kuching, with trips to surrounding areas of interest, including an orang-utan sanctuary, national parks, beaches and Iban and Bidayuh longhouses.

1. The Essential Kuching

This half-day tour takes in many of the highlights of Sarawak's capital, giving you the afternoon to take it easy around the hotel pool. If you're pressed for time, however, you can combine it with the subsequent itinerary for a jam-packed day in one of Southeast Asia's most delightful cities.

Begin early in the morning at the far end of the **Kuching Waterfront**, where the panorama from the top of the **Lookout Tower** includes the **Astana**, the State Mosque and the old town of Kuching, with Mount

Santubong visible in the distance as you face the river, and Gunung Serapi on the horizon to your left. The Astana, on the site of James Brooke's residence, was built in 1870 by the second White Rajah, Charles, as a wedding gift to his wife, Margaret. Now the official residence of Sarawak's Governor, it is not open to the public.

The Astana – now the Governor's residence

After you've descended the tower, pass the fountain courtyard to the aptly named **Square Tower**, built in 1879 to guard the town (the guns were never fired in defence). Across the road from this fortress stands the gracious **Court House**, an exquisitely

proportioned series of white colonnaded buildings topped by *belian* or ironwood tiles. Built in 1874 to house the government offices, it is used today as the seat of the High Court in Borneo (the Supreme Court of Sarawak). In front of the Court House is the stone **Charles Brooke Memorial**, its four embossed bronze plaques representing Sarawak's European, Malay, Iban and Chinese races.

Behind the court is the **Round Tower**, planned as a fort but never used as such, with an adjacent wedding cake of a building known as the **Pavilion**. This strange structure, once used as a hospital, is currently undergoing renovation and will eventually re-open as a costume museum.

Cross the road and pass the **post office**, its Corinthian columns typical of a Victorian pseudo-Greek building. You are now at the end of Jalan Carpenter, and breakfast is just ahead. Although you're about to plunge into Chinatown, the first building on your right is the popular Indian Muslim **National Islamic Café**, where you can get a good *roti canai*. However, I recommend keeping on for about 50 m (55 yards), until you come to a small Chinese temple, where writhing dragons form the handles of a pair of stunning brass incense burners. Immediately opposite is a roofed courtyard with a collection of food stalls set in front of a stage topped with a pagoda-like roof. Once used for the performance of Chinese opera, this area now offers several types of Chinese cuisine.

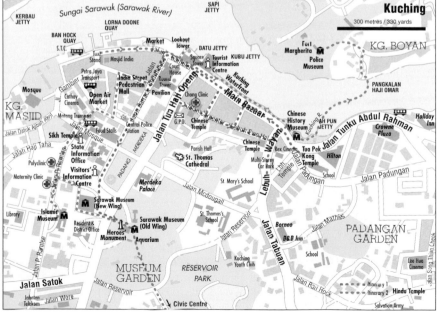

The Tua Pek Kong temple

If you like a rich pork soup with fresh rice-flour noodles and boiled egg, order *kueh cap* at the stall on your left as you face the stage (the stall is taken over by another cook at around 11am, when it sells prawn noodles), or try the *laksa*, or pork porridge, from other stalls. Suitably fortified, continue your stroll down Jalan Carpenter, taking time to sidetrack up and down the very short **Jalan China** and **Jalan Bishopgate**. To the sound of tinsmiths beating noisily and food sizzling in coffee shop woks, wander past provision shops and Chinese medicine halls, acupuncturists and vendors of basketware, cheap and cheerful furniture stores and gleaming goldsmiths' shops, tailors and clan association buildings.

Jalan Carpenter changes its name for no appreciable reason to Jalan Ewe Hai before ending at Lebuh Wayang. Cross this street and turn left; when you come to Main Bazaar, running opposite the Waterfront, turn right and head for the **Tua Pek Kong** temple on a small hillock. Built in the 1840s on the confluence of the Mata Kuching (from which the city got its name) and Sarawak rivers, Kuching's oldest temple enjoys excellent *feng shui* and attracts crowds of worshippers.

Opposite, you'll see the **Chinese History Museum**, one of the two original buildings still standing along the river (the other is the **Sarawak Steamship Building**, near the Square Tower); the rest were demolished to create the Kuching Waterfront park in 1994. This museum is included in the next itinerary, and it's now time to let shopping mania take over as you walk along **Main Bazaar**. This was once

Chinatown labourer

dominated by vendors of such basics as hardware and foodstuffs, but today the curio and antique dealers almost outnumber the other stores (see *Shopping*, page 62). Browse and buy to your heart's content, pausing to look at the shops selling processed birds' nests and nicely packaged Sarawak pepper. If you fancy, you could have an Iban motif tattooed by the modern (less painful) electric process at 24 Main Bazaar. As you pass Seng Kee Produce (1983), the smell of pepper will catch your throat; sacks of black and white peppercorns sit on the cement floor, with the current prices chalked up on a blackboard.

Before leaving Main Bazaar, pause for a cool drink at one of the coffee shops. Turn left up Jalan Courthouse, pass the cheerful blue-painted police station and the Visitors' Information Centre on the right of the Padang Merdeka (Open Square) and you'll arrive at the new wing of the **Sarawak Museum** (open daily, 9am–6pm), one of the oldest and best museums in Southeast Asia, founded by Charles Brooke in 1891. Before you go into the new wing, take a look at the stunning carved funerary poles (keliriang) in the garden. The ground floor of the New Wing has a good gift shop with the best range of Borneo books in town and an historical section with interesting lithographs, paintings and photographs. The ethnographic collection is upstairs. Apart from photographs of Sarawak's different tribal groups and a distribution map, there is a series of recreations of longhouse interiors, as well as a simple Penan dwelling.

A stall in Main Bazaar

Cooking, agricultural and hunting implements are on display, plus costumes, musical instruments and superb Iban textiles. The magnificent storage jars which form part of the ceramic collection are also worth studying.

The architecture of the old wing, reached by a pedestrian bridge crossing busy Jalan Tun Haji Openg, was supposedly inspired by a house in Normandy. The inside is entirely Sarawakian, however. One of the joys of this old wing is that you're never quite sure what you'll see next. A stuffed orang-utan is not far from a model of an antimony mine; a hair ball and a pair of spectacles retrieved from a crocodile's stomach can be found near a display of shells. Upstairs, models of longhouses and displays of handicrafts are set off by the dramatic Tree of Life mural painted by the late Tusau Padan, a famous Kenyah artist. Check out the section on tattooing, and if the subject intrigues you, the infamous *palang*, or penis pin. The museum is so fascinating that only your stomach insisting it's lunch time will make you leave.

You get a look at a traditional Malay kampung, a British fort, Indian Muslim and Chinese shopping areas, Chinese and Islamic museums and a stroll through tropical gardens to the Civic Centre in this varied half-day itinerary.

If you haven't already had lunch, you could try the air-conditioned **A La Carte** food court in the basement of the Lebuh Wayang car

park, or have something light and healthy at **Life Café**, nearby in Jalan Ewe Hai. Escape from the heat of midday while visiting the **Chinese History Museum** (open daily, 9am–6pm), across from the Tua Pek Kong temple. Once used by the Chinese Chamber of Commerce, the museum consists of a single exhibition hall where a number of artefacts (a gilded chariot for carrying religious statues, an old trishaw, porcelain) are joined by displays of photographs,

A tambang ferry

maps and information panels tracing the history of the Chinese in Sarawak. You'll learn a lot, not just about famous personalities but also why certain industries and crafts are dominated by one particular dialect group.

Come out of the museum and a little to your left is the jetty for Pangkalan Haji Omar, where you can catch one of the typical *tambang* ferries across to **Kampung Boyan** and **Fort Margherita**. It'll take a couple of minutes and a mere 30 sen to cross the river (you can hire a *tambang* to take you on a river cruise for around RM15 for 30 minutes). Walk up the stone steps and into a different era in Kampung Boyan, a typical Malay village where wooden houses, many festooned with pots of orchids, cluster among fruit trees. Absorb the atmosphere of this traditional village, then return to your starting point and turn left at the sign "Muz(i)um Poli(s)". Keep go-

ing left, following a high wire-mesh fence around a two-storey building until you enter the police compound. Go up the hill, cross the parade ground (still keeping left), then go downhill until you reach the entrance to Fort Margherita (open daily, 9am–6pm). Climb the spiral staircase of the quaint tower (built in 1879) to see the quirky collection of weapons and police memorabilia, including fascinating material and photographs relating to the communist insurgency of the 1960s. You

Fort Margherita

Bustling Jalan India

can also climb to the gun emplacements and walk around the ramparts, which give a splendid view back over the city.

Return by ferry to the Kuching Waterfront, strolling along until you reach **Jalan Gambier**. Walk up past the three buildings of the market; the first, housing fresh vegetables and dry goods, is worth exploring; the second contains the fish market and is usually a little challenging to enter, but do look at the unusual curving verandah covered with *belian* tiles. Pass the poultry market, cross the road and come back down past the row of bustling Indian Muslim provision shops, a riot of spices and plastic bags of oil, mounds of margarine and sacks of chillies.

Turn up into Jalan Courthouse, and about 25m (27 yards) along this road you'll find yourself at the start of **Jalan India**, a pedestrian mall that is the heart of the Muslim area of town. Fabric stores predominate, but the people are generally more interesting than the produce. Pause next to No 39, where you'll find a tiny corridor leading to Sarawak's oldest **Indian Muslim mosque**, built in the 1850s.

When you turn out of Jalan India into **Lorong Kai Joo**, you suddenly plunge from Muslim India into China. This lane, once notorious for its Chinese brothels, has some fascinating small shops – No 12, for example, houses a coffin maker who also fashions paper houses, cars and other objects for ritual burning so that they will accompany the deceased into the underworld. Opposite is an excellent bakery, famous for its curry puffs.

Cross the busy road in front of you, turn right, then take the first left. Continue along this road, passing the attractive Sikh temple on your left, until you come into Jalan P Ramlee (named after the popular Malay singer, actor and film director who made hearts throb during the 1950s and 1960s). The **Sarawak Islamic Museum** claims fame as the first Islamic museum established in Southeast Asia. A converted 1930s Malay college building reproduces the serenity found in Middle Eastern interior courtyards and gardens, providing much of the museum's appeal. The contents, grouped into seven galleries, depict the Islamic heritage of the Muslim

The Civic Centre

community both locally and abroad. The provenance of many of the exhibits is frustratingly vague, but there are sufficient interesting items, including pottery, decorative arts, textiles and weaponry, to make the museum worth a visit.

Go back down P Ramlee and opposite the clinic take the road leading up to the new wing of the **Sarawak Museum**. Cross the pedestrian bridge to the old wing, where, around the back next to the public toilets, is the pretty little wrought-iron pavilion housing the **Aquarium**. Not a great deal of interest here, except for the Arawana fish, which can fetch over RM1,000 for the gold-scaled variety, thought by the Chinese to confer fortune on the owner.

The museum gardens, gently sculpted with a rotunda and park benches, are reminiscent of an English park until you see the fragrant frangipani, flamboyant palm trees and old circular Chinese tombstones. Cross the gardens diagonally until you come to Jalan Taman Budaya and head down to the busy roundabout. Turn right up Jalan Budaya and when you reach the private Sarawak Club, cross the road to the **Civic Centre** (Kompleks Dewan Suarah). Take the glass-walled lift up to the lookout tower (level 3) for a spectacular 360° view out over Kuching and the surrounding countryside, which is most remarkable at sunset.

To get back downtown, walk past the Sarawak Club down to Jalan Tun Haji Openg, cross the road and wait at the bus stop for your short ride.

Sunset view from the Civic Centre

3. Meeting the Man of the Forest

Take an early-morning or post-lunch trip to the Semenggoh Wildlife Rehabilitation Centre to meet the orang-utan or 'man of the forest'. Explore some of the forest trails and pause at a pottery on the way back to see how the distinctive local ceramics are created.

The star attraction at this centre for the rehabilitation of wild animals – set inside the 740-hectare (1,828-acre) **Semenggoh Forest Reserve** – is the orang-utan, which is found in the wild only in Borneo and Sumatra. The intelligence of this huge, gentle ape and its remarkably human expressions make it a source of endless fascination. Perhaps it's not surprising that the animal's Malay name, *orang-utan*, means 'man of the forest'.

The day before you visit the **Wildlife Centre** – just 32 km/20 miles south of Kuching – pick up a free entry permit from the Visitors' Information Centre (open daily, 8am–4.15pm) in Kuching, next to the Sarawak Museum (open Monday to Thursday, 8am–4.15; Friday, 8am–4.45pm; Saturday, 8am–12.45pm). This will allow you to arrive at Semenggoh by 8am, giving you plenty of time to watch the orang-utans come in from the forest for their morning meal at around 8.30am. The mornings are cooler – if you can call 26°C (78°F) rather than 32°C (89°F) cool! – and there's more likelihood of seeing birds in the surrounding forest. If you are only able to make this trip in the afternoon, be sure to get there well in advance of feeding time at 3pm. Don't forget to pack your mosquito repellent, because you're going to need it.

Feeding time for an orang-utan

I recommend hiring a taxi to take you to Semenggoh, asking the driver to wait while you visit, and then stopping at the pottery on the way back to Kuching. The current charge is RM60 for the return journey, with RM10 per hour for waiting time, and the taxi is permitted to drive right up to the entrance of the rehabilitation centre. If you're on a tight budget, or prefer to go by bus, catch the 7am STC bus No 6 from the end of Jalan Gambier, near the mosque, and ask the driver to let you off at the Forest Department Nursery in Semenggoh. From here, it's about a 20-minute walk along a sealed road through the forest to the rehabilitation centre; don't forget your hat as there's no shade along here. For an afternoon visit, take the bus leaving Kuching at 1.20pm. Buses back to Kuching pass the entrance of the Forest Department Nursery

Swinging down for lunch

at 10.30am, 1pm, 3.15pm and 4pm, although it is possible to walk 20–30 minutes through Kampung Jawa to the main Kuching–Serian highway and catch any bus back from there.

The rehabilitation centre was established in 1975 with the object of training captive animals to fend for themselves so that they can be released back into the forest. It is strictly against the law to keep most mammals – and especially orang-utans – in captivity in Malaysia, yet sometimes babies taken captive when their mothers have been killed, as well as animals which have been injured, are still brought to Semenggoh. After a thorough medical check, the animals are gradually introduced to the forest, while being given nourishment in the form of milk, fruit, seeds and sugar cane.

As the orang-utans become better at finding their own food, they visit the feeding area less frequently. Sometimes during the fruiting season they can find all they need in the forest and don't come to the feeding area at all. This can be frustrating for the tourists who've come to watch them, but it's a sure sign that their rehabilitation has been a success.

The orang-utan, being an ape, has no tail. Unlike the gibbon, which moves quickly through the forest by swinging like a pendulum on its long arms, the heavier orang-utan moves slowly and deliberately. When it is near feeding time, visitors go along the boardwalks

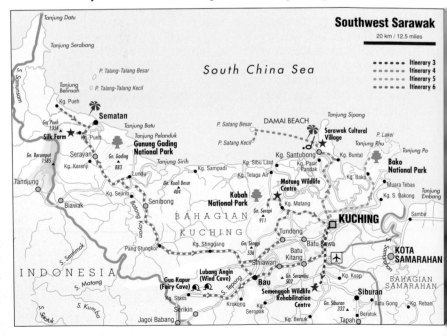

to a roped-off area near the feeding platform, where the ranger sets out food and calls the animals by name. If you're fortunate, you'll see several orang-utans descend from the nearby trees to grab a bunch of bananas or slurp milk from a bucket.

Apart from these semi-wild creatures, several recalcitrant orang-utans which refuse to be rehabilitated or are considered dangerous are kept in a large cage at the centre. There are also cages with sun bears pacing endlessly back and forth in boredom, some deer, a lonely-looking proboscis monkey and a furry gibbon or two in separate cages. One of the two large bird enclosures has a striking rhinoceros hornbill, the Sarawak state emblem.

Crested fireback pheasant

If seeing animals in captivity upsets you, move quickly past this area and out to the marked forest trails. (At the time of writing, **Matang Wildlife Centre**, set in the Kubah National Park, was being constructed to house captive animals in an open-concept 'zoo'. As it is uncertain whether the animals at Semenggoh will be transferred there, check with the Visitors' Information Centre in Kuching.)

The Semenggoh Forest Reserve is an area of primary rainforest, so if you're not going to be spending time in any of Sarawak's national parks, it's a good idea to walk along some of the trails and see the giant dipterocarp trees, various jungle fruit trees, rattan vines, orchids, palms and so forth.

About 12 km (7½ miles) away from Semenggoh, on the highway back to Kuching, there are a couple of **potteries** on the left, not far beyond the Shell station. Kuching's potteries, all Chinese-owned (with the artisans almost invariably Teochew), were initially located near a clay bed closer to town and produced functional items such as water storage jars, cooking pots and pots for steaming medicinal herbs. Now they concentrate largely on items for the tourist trade, often decorated with traditional tribal motifs. Some of the stuff is sheer kitsch, but other items are appealing and all are inexpensive.

The best-known pottery, **Ng Hua Seng**, is located here (next to Yong Huat Heng). You are free to wander around the workshop area and watch the potters at work. You can then browse among the results in the shop, and if you decide on something impractically large, don't worry: all the potteries are accustomed to shipping goods overseas.

Adding the finishing touches

The Damai Beach resort

4. Sarawak Cultural Village and Damai

The award-winning Sarawak Cultural Village, nestling under Mount Santubong, is your first stop on a day of discovery. You can then laze on the beach at Satang Island, take a hike, rent a mountain bike or play golf. After a feast of seafood at Buntal fishing village, either return to Kuching or stay overnight at Damai.

The forest-covered mountains of the Santubong peninsula, guarding the entrance to the Sarawak river, form a glorious backdrop to **Damai Beach**, 35km (22 miles) and around 40 minutes from downtown Kuching. Apart from three resort hotels with their wide range of recreational facilities, there is an 18-hole golf course designed by US golfer Arnold Palmer, fishing villages, hiking trails and nearby **Satang Island**.

If you plan on staying overnight at Damai, book your accommodation in advance and ask the resort's recreation desk to arrange for a boat to transfer you to Satang at about 1pm. Holiday Inn manages two resorts here, Damai Beach and Damai Lagoon. I prefer the hilltop 'longhouse' rooms at the Damai Beach resort for their stunning views, as well as the glorious clifftop swimming pool (see 'Accommodation', page 80). If you don't plan to make an overnight stay, book your return boat trip to Satang Island with Matahari Tours at the Holiday Inn Kuching (tel: 082 247709). The transfer to Satang costs around RM70 per person for a minimum of two passengers.

To get to Damai Beach, take the 9am shuttle bus from the Holiday Inn Kuching – check that departure times have not been changed (tel: 082 423111). The fare at present is RM10 one way; ask the driver to let you off at the **Sarawak Cultural Village**. The entrance fee (currently RM45 for adults, RM22.50 for children) includes

Sarawak Cultural Village

a cultural show, which is held twice daily in the comfortable, air-conditioned theatre.

Located between the two Holiday Inn resorts, the Sarawak Cultural Village fully deserves the praise that has been lavished on it. Seven different ethnic communities are highlighted in this 'living museum', where traditional dwellings are located around a small lake set in 7 hectares (17 acres) of land. If you travel clockwise around the lake, your first stop will be at the Chinese farmhouse, an authentic recreation of a typical house, right down to the radio, bicycle and thermos flask. You can see how birds' nests are processed and learn about pepper cultivation, which the Chinese established in Sarawak.

The homes and longhouses of the Malay, Melanau, Orang Ulu, Penan, Iban and Bidayuh are all equally authentic; look for the maps on each house showing the location of that particular ethnic group, and read the interesting information panels. Surprisingly, the occupants of each dwelling – who have come from their own villages or remote longhouses to live at the village – don't seem jaded by welcoming so many visitors, and retain a remarkable freshness and genuine friendliness. The same is true of the thoroughly professional performers in the cultural show.

When the morning show finishes, pause at the Cultural Village restaurant for a quick lunch, unless you've brought a picnic from Kuching. Buy plenty of cool drinks and then walk to the Holiday Inn Damai Beach for your boat transfer to Satang Island. There are actually two islands, the larger being **Satang Besar**, where green turtles come ashore at night to lay their eggs. You can snorkel, swim and enjoy the white sandy beach here. During the north-

The cultural show

east monsoon season (especially December and January), sea conditions may make it inadvisable to go to Satang, but there are plenty of alternatives for the afternoon.

You could do a jungle trek on the slopes of **Mount Santubong**. The marked trail is quite easy, with only one short, steep stretch, and takes you across small streams through typical lowland rainforest for about 1½ to 2 hours. The trail starts behind the Santubong Mountain Trek Canteen and comes out onto the road near the Cultural Village. Don't confuse this trail with the very demanding, 6-hour trek to the summit. Alternatively, go past the Damai Lagoon resort to the **Damai Rainforest Resort**, where there's a circular trail through the forest. The resort's waterfront restaurant is a lovely place to stop for a drink at the end of your trek.

If you enjoy golf, you could have a round at the beautifully situated **Damai Golf Course**, where you can hire everything from golf clubs to shoes. At present, green fees for 18 holes are around RM150 on weekdays and RM180 on weekends (tel: 082 846088 for further information and bookings).

Mountain bikes can be hired from either of the Holiday Inn resorts for about RM15 per hour. Once you've got over a couple of challenging hills, it's an enjoyable ride to **Kampung Santubong**, a Malay fishing village. Pause en route to walk up to the **Damai Lookout Point**, clearly marked on the left of the road before the turnoff to Santubong, for a view down over the bay. If it's clear, you can see as far as Tanjung Datu, the point marking the border with West Kalimantan (Indonesia).

If you just want to laze around at the poolside, however, and are not staying the night at Holiday Inn's Damai Beach resort, pay for a day-visit pass, which entitles you to use the restaurants and swimming pools. For the ultimate in relaxation, listen to the sound of the waves as you enjoy a traditional Malay massage between the main swimming pool and the beach. The beach itself, it must be admitted, doesn't really invite swimming.

Enjoying a meal

Ask the resort to arrange transport to **Kampung Buntal** for your dinner. Kampung Buntal is a Malay fishing village on the edge of the bay strung between Santubong and Bako peninsulas. The sunset from one of the basic wooden seafood restaurants is often superb. The major restaurants are all Chinese-owned and my favourite (and, apparently, the favourite of dozens of Kuching residents who flock here every evening) is **Lim Hok Ann**, which your driver is sure to know. The jumble of drink cases and provisions crowding the front of the cavernous restaurant reflects the very Chinese attitude that ambience is all very well, but in a restaurant it's only the food that matters.

Provided the weather is good, the tables will be set out on the open wooden platform near the water's edge. Ask for a mosquito coil if you haven't brought repellent, then set about the serious business of ordering. I've never seen a menu here – diners just ask for what they want (crabs, squid, fish, vegetables, etc) and then specify how they want it cooked. Don't miss the restaurant's excellent version of one of Malaysia's best cross-cultural dishes: butter prawns, fried to a crisp and flavoured with Indian curry leaves. I also like the bamboo clams (*ambal*), a Sarawak speciality, cooked with garlic, squid fried with dried chillies (not as hot and spicy as it sounds) and steamed fish. The slender *midin* fern, with its asparagus-like taste and texture, is a must. You should expect to pay around RM20–25 per person, excluding drinks, and you must bring cash because credit cards are not accepted.

Riding in a longboat

5. Beauty and Beasts at Bako

Despite being the second smallest park in Sarawak, Bako, just over an hour from Kuching, offers a better chance of seeing wildlife than any other national park. A great variety of terrain is packed into this tiny gem of a place, as well as some lovely beaches. This is a two-day itinerary, which could well be extended.

Although it's possible to take a day trip to Bako, I strongly recommend spending at least one night there. Book accommodation at the Visitors' Information Centre in Kuching and try to avoid going at the weekend when Bako gets packed with day trippers. Leave Kuching as early as possible and take the air-conditioned bus No 6 to Bako from near the covered food stalls (confusingly known as the 'open market') in front of Electra House. If you miss the bus, which departs roughly every hour, take one of the frequent minibuses (kereta sewa) from the same area, or hire a taxi.

In about 45 minutes, having crossed the Sarawak river and headed north through new industrial estates, you'll reach **Kampung Bako**. Check in with your booking slip at the reception centre beside the river, and see if there are any other visitors with whom you can share the cost of a longboat to the park. If you haven't come equipped with drinks and food for a picnic lunch (you can buy bread rolls at the Hilton's basement coffee shop and other food at Parkson Grand supermarket in the basement of the Riverside Complex), stock up at the Chinese restaurant opposite

It takes about 20 minutes to travel down the Bako river and along the coast to the jetty near the park headquarters. When you arrive, arrange with the boatman to wait for about half an hour while you check in and leave your bags, then return for a trip to the beach at **Telok Pandan Kecil**. The boatman will probably ask for around RM25 one way, but you can try haggling. (You could also arrange with him to be picked up from the park in the afternoon, or you could take a chance on finding a departing boat you can share back to Kampung Bako.) On your way to the beach, you'll pass the famous **Sea Stacks**, tall stone structures standing

33

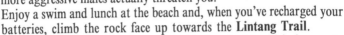

in the sea and sculpted by the wind and waves into fantastic shapes, with colourful patterns created by minerals.

Telok Pandan Kecil is an idyllic spot (although the sea can get rough during the northeast monsoon between December and February), with a small river running into the bay. Be sure to have your picnic lunch in a securely fastened bag and don't leave anything small lying around on the beach – the macaque monkeys here and around the park headquarters cease to be cute when they steal your food, or when some of the more aggressive males actually threaten you. Enjoy a swim and lunch at the beach and, when you've recharged your batteries, climb the rock face up towards the **Lintang Trail**.

You'll cross a strange plateau of pitted rock slabs with dry scrub, a moonscape quite unlike anything else you're likely to encounter in Sarawak. This *padang*, as it is known, is full of carnivorous pitcher plants and can be very hot, so you'll need a sunhat and water bottle. When you come to the Lintang Trail, turn right and head towards the park headquarters. Follow this until you take a right turn onto the **Teluk Paku Trail**, where you'll see some superb rattans and vines and, if it's late afternoon and you're very quiet, maybe some proboscis monkeys. These strange, pot-bellied, long-nosed monkeys are found only in Borneo; they can leap prodigious distances (usually very noisily) and even swim. You may see them along the trail or down on the beach at Teluk Paku.

Back again on the main Lintang Trail, you'll descend a very steep hill and arrive at swampy **Teluk Asam**, a fascinating spot to sit (drenched in mosquito repellent) in the hides at low tide and watch fiddler crabs, birds and sometimes proboscis monkeys and otters.

Have dinner at the canteen; there's no beer available but the range of cooked food is adequate and they have a well-stocked store where you can get everything from mosquito coils to rubber thongs. If you want to see a nature video at 8pm, arrange it when you check in. There's not much else to do at night, apart from keeping an eye open for the ungainly, timid bearded pigs which hunt around the canteen looking for food.

Pitcher plant

The next morning, get up at around 6am and walk along the trail towards **Teluk Delima**. You pass through some magnificent dipterocarp rainforest and may spot squirrels, tree shrews, silver leaf monkeys, proboscis monkeys and colugos (known as flying lemurs, although they're not primates and are unrelated to anything else in the animal kingdom). In the early morning, you have a good chance of seeing hornbills, racket-tailed drongos, tailor birds and magpie robins. At low tide, the swampy foreshore of Teluk Delima is sometimes visited by proboscis monkeys. The best way to detect their presence in the forest is to sit quietly for some time and listen for their clumsy crashing.

After breakfast, wander through the **interpretation centre**, which concentrates on the geology, flora and fauna of Bako. There are plenty of other trails you can explore, even though the entire northeast portion of Bako National Park has been closed for some time. The **Tajor Waterfall**, reached via the Lintang and Tajor trails, is a pretty spot provided it's not too dry (check with the rangers first). You must check out of your accommodation at 11am, but can leave your bag at the administration centre until your time of departure. You may be tempted to stay another night. With its peace, beauty and richly varied environment, Bako is that kind of place.

6. Exploring the First Division

The bucolic hills west of Kuching are home to limestone caves, three national parks (one renowned for the world's largest flower), Sarawak's best beaches and the Bidayuh or Land Dyaks. Discover this seldom-visited region in a two-day, one-night itinerary.

Despite recent surfacing of the once-dreadful road heading west to Lundu and Sematan, few tourists visit this delightful region of Sarawak. Although it's officially known as the **Kuching Division**, most locals still call it by its old name, the First Division, as this was the Sarawak ruled by James Brooke.

You can hire a car for this trip, or if you prefer to have a driver/guide, contact Saga Tours or one of the other recommended tour operators (*see page 86*). Before you leave Kuching, make a booking to stay overnight at the **Gunung Gading National Park**, which has two chalets and four four-bed hostel rooms.

Head south of Kuching on the road towards Serian; just past the airport turnoff, at the well-marked roundabout, turn right in the direction of Bau. You're quickly in the countryside with rice paddies

First Division exploration

The home of 'Sarawak's Sultan'

and fruit trees, the abrupt, forest-covered limestone hills of Bau visible on the horizon. Shortly before you reach Bau, you'll come to the atmospheric old Chinese bazaar of **Siniawan** with coffee shops, pork butchers and birds'-nest traders. Pause at Hao & Hao Coffee Shop (No 22) for a bowl of breakfast noodles and absorb the tranquil pace of life. If you want to see the painstaking process of cleaning birds' nests, go into No 19, where Lam Chin Jee is most helpful.

There is little of interest in the town of **Bau**, once an important centre for gold mining, apart from the attractive **Civic Centre** or Dewan Suarah, in the shape of a Bidayuh *baruk*, or head house. Go through Bau, turn right towards Lundu/Sematan, then turn left after the large Chinese graveyard (the sign reads 'SMK Lake'). Keep going until you see the sign for **Lubang Angin – Wind Cave**. At the entrance, near the river, you can hire a torch and walk through the cave passage, which will take about 40 minutes. For another – and actually more interesting – cave, come back to the main road, turn right and follow the signs for **Gua Kapur – Fairy Cave**.

You'll pass a wacky collection of ramshackle wooden buildings decorated with coats-of-arms, the home of an eccentric local who proclaims himself 'Sultan of Sarawak'. Keep going until you see the sign for Fairy Cave, which can be reached via a cement staircase. The trail through it (allow about an hour) is dotted with a number of small shrines.

Head back towards Bau and follow the signs in the direction of Lundu/Sematan. The road winds through gentle countryside marked with cocoa and pepper fields, fish ponds, fruit trees, quarries and a large *Acacia mangium* softwood plantation. Some 3km (2 miles) from Lundu is the vehicular ferry crossing, a real bottleneck at weekends and holidays; avoid such times or expect to wait 2–3 hours.

Shortly before you get into **Lundu**, a peaceful town on the river, turn at the sign towards Siar and Pandan beach. On the left, just

Fishing boats at anchor

past the notice for Lundu Water Treatment Plant, is a discreet little sign for Gunung Gading National Park. Check in and have a look at the **information centre** in the attractive Bidayuh building before heading into Lundu town for lunch. The food stall at the end beside the bright red Tua Pek Kong temple cooks to order; the fish is very fresh, and the noodles and veggie dishes are also good.

From Lundu it's just 27km (17 miles) to **Sematan**, the last sizeable village before the border with Kalimantan at Tanjung Datu. Sizeable is a relative term: Sematan is little more than a lodging house, a market and a few stalls, provision stores and coffee shops. A jetty juts out into the estuary, where fishing boats come in with the tide – all very picturesque and peaceful. If the tide is in and you're in the mood for a swim, take the road west, past the police station, and then travel 2–3km (1–2 miles) along the dirt road that skirts the coast. There are several short trails through coconut plantations or past melon patches to the lovely long beach which is generally deserted. The sand shelves so gradually that you have to walk some distance into the wonderfully clean sea before being able to swim, with a view towards the hills of Tanjung Datu.

Return to Sematan and take the road back in the direction of Lundu. You'll see

Displaying the catch

a right turn marked **Kampung Pueh**. Travel along this road until you see the sign for a mulberry plantation where silkworms are raised and their silk prepared. Although there aren't any official arrangements for visitors, the staff are generally very helpful if you just turn up and ask to look around.

Go back towards Sematan and turn right at the Rumah Adat Kampung Pueh sign. About 50m (55 yards) down this road is the last remaining traditional Bidayuh longhouse in the Lundu district. The Bidayuh are made up of a collection of related groups and those living in this region are known as Selakau. They tend to be reticent in contrast with the extrovert, friendly Iban. Although they have a visitors' book and request a donation of RM10 from visitors to the longhouse, the Selakau of Kampung Pueh show little interest in tourism and overnight visits are not catered for. You can explore the verandah, where the boxed-in platforms are the traditional sleeping quarters for the bachelors of the longhouse, and where a large wooden mortar for husking rice stands outside each family's private quarters. You may see a few older people weaving baskets but most of the younger generation have left the longhouse.

Head back towards Lundu for dinner, then spend the night at Gunung Gading. The next morning, it's time to explore some of the trails of this delightful park, famous for its *Rafflesia priceii* sites, where the world's largest flower — growing up to 1m (over 3 ft) in diameter — can often be seen. Ask the park staff if there's a *rafflesia* flowering; it's well worth the hike up the mountain slopes to see this strange, fleshy bloom. According to legend, Gunung Gading (Ivory Mountain) is named after a Javanese princess who used to bath at one of the glorious waterfalls. A more prosaic explanation is that it's named after the illipe nut, known as *engkabang gading*, which grows in abundance.

Rafflesia in bloom

The trails are all steep, but well worth tackling to visit one of the waterfalls. Waterfall 7 has a series of cascades but, for swimming and sheer beauty, my choice is Waterfall 3 (it's also closer). When you've finished enjoying Gunung Gading, start heading back towards Kuching. You could also go swimming at **Pandan beach**, just 10 minutes away.

Shortly before reaching Bau, take the Singgai road left towards **Kubah National Park**; this road skirts the village of Tundong and travels through pretty countryside and Bidayuh farms, with Gunung Serapi on your left, until it comes out on the main road to Kubah (marked Sg China Matang). Much of this region is preserved within the 2,230-hectare (5,500-acre) Kubah National Park. The luxurious, beautifully situated chalets here (currently RM160 a night) are the best value in Sarawak, and the park itself is well known for its pretty waterfalls and varied forest, including a large number of palms. You may be tempted to spend the night here, just a short drive from the **Matang Wildlife Centre** (to open shortly) and a mere 20km (12 miles) from Kuching.

7. Staying with the Iban of Ulu Ai

No visit to Sarawak would be complete without a night or two in an Iban longhouse. Drive to the lake created by the Batang Ai Dam and journey upriver by longboat through rapids and rainforest to Ulu Ai for a couple of nights in the heart of Borneo.

— Several major tour operators have an exclusive arrangement with a particular longhouse in the Batang Ai or Skrang region. My favourite is Borneo Adventure's Rumah Along at Nanga Sumpa, ideal for discovering longhouse life in a region totally undisturbed by commercial logging. Borneo Adventure (see p86 for details) has built a lodge adjacent to the 28-door longhouse, ensuring privacy for both the Iban and their visitors. An alternative to Nanga Sumpa is Borneo Adventure's smaller lodge at Wong Tibu longhouse, almost on the border of the vast Batang Ai National Park — N.B. Be sure to take gifts for your hosts (see p76). —

A Nanga Sumpa longhouse resident

Your tour guide will pick you up early for the 4-hour drive to the **Batang Ai Dam**. You'll probably pause at the town of **Serian** for a quick noodle breakfast and a visit to the colourful market, where you may see sago worms (reportedly delicious barbecued) wriggling in a bucket. There are many pepper farms in this district, so if you're interested in a quick look and a purchase, ask your driver to stop.

You could have an early lunch at one of the restaurants serving tasty duck rice at Lachau but, if you can wait an hour, ask the driver to take you to **Engkilili**, a sleepy little town on the banks of the Batang Lupar just five minutes off the road. Joo Huat, No 31 on the road facing the river, has an excellent cook; try his crispy noodles.

When you arrive at the Batang Ai Hydroelectric Dam, you'll transfer to a longboat for the 2-hour trip across the huge lake and up the river to Nanga Sumpa. (The Hilton Batang Ai Longhouse resort has a rest stop with clean toilets on the hill above the jetty.) The lake formed by the huge dam is not an attractive sight during drier times of the year, when thousands of dead trees protrude starkly from the water. After about an hour you'll be into the **Engkari**, then heading up the Delok river, which is surrounded by virgin rainforest. If the river level is low, you may have to leave your longboat at the base of a small waterfall and wade along the river's edge past the falls. Watch the Iban casually shoulder a huge outboard engine or your luggage and trot barefoot across the rocks to where empty longboats are waiting and you'll have enormous respect for their strength and sense of balance.

When you finally arrive at Nanga Sumpa, it can be almost an anticlimax if you're expecting the sort of picture-postcard longhouse you'll see at the Sarawak Cultural Village. Viewed from the river, the longhouse is partly obscured. The notched tree trunk which acts as the entrance stairway faces the little Sumpa river which separates the longhouse from the visitors' lodge. It is normal for a

Life in the longhouse

traditional welcome ceremony, or *miring*, to be performed when guests arrive but, as most people are working in their fields during the day, this will probably be held in the evening. Relax at the simple but comfortable lodge (mattresses, mosquito nets and proper toilets provided), or cool off with a swim in the river.

After dinner, it's time to make a formal visit to the longhouse. You will probably now enjoy the *miring*, which involves the setting out of ceremonial foods and *tuak* (rice wine), with the waving of a rooster and chanted prayers. The gifts you have brought will be handed to the children, who are expected to do a dance for you.

An Iban dancer

You may have noticed women weaving at a backstrap loom on the verandah, or *ruai*, of the longhouse earlier in the day. At night, you'll have a chance to buy their hand-woven fabric, as well as cloth made in other longhouses.

Life in the longhouse is very democratic, with each family maintaining its own quarters as well as the portion of communal verandah in front of their *bilek*. (This is why you'll notice a great difference in the state of repair of the *ruai*.) Remember, only go into a *bilek* if you are invited. You can buy bottles of *tuak* for RM3 each; it's appreciated if you buy a few extra bottles and give them to your hosts. Don't forget the women — they enjoy a glass of *tuak* as well. If the party gets going, you may be treated to a drumming contest, or a dance which culminates in the dancer picking up a glass of *tuak* from the floor with his teeth, drinking the contents, putting the glass back and continuing to dance.

After a comfortable night's rest in the lodge, you'll be feeling ready for a little upriver adventure, including a barbecue picnic on the shingle bed not far from **Wong Ensulai Waterfall**. You can trek up with your guide (about 1½ hours) if you wish, but I prefer to travel by boat as you get a clearer view of the forest. En route, you'll stop several times while the Iban fell a thorny palm, inspect a clump of bamboo for edible young shoots, gather wild ferns and fragrant *illipe* leaves and cut lengths of bamboo into cooking tubes.

Take a plunge in the refreshing waters of the waterfall, then dry off on the shingle bed as you watch for butterflies and birds and smell your lunch cooking in bamboo tubes over the fire. You may even catch sight of a wild orang-utan while you wait; the best sighting I've ever had of this magnificent ape was here in Ulu Ai.

Sibu & Central Sarawak

Sibu is the gateway to the longhouses of the Rajang river and the coastal region around Mukah. North of Sibu, en route for Bintulu, the Kakus and Kemena rivers and their tributaries also have many longhouses. To reach Sibu from Kuching, take either an express boat (roughly 4 hours; *see page 78*) or a plane (*see page 77*). The airport is about 30 minutes out of Sibu and a taxi (the only transport) costs RM20. If you are coming from the north, you can either fly from Miri or Bintulu to Sibu, or take an express bus which links all three towns.

8. Up the Rajang River

—Travel up Sarawak's greatest river to Kapit, the last outpost, then move on to a luxurious longhouse resort near the famous Pelagus Rapids for a delightful introduction to life along the Rajang. This is your base for a couple of nights as you explore the rainforest, visit a nearby Iban longhouse and take a dip in a jungle pool. Don't forget to take your swimsuit.—

If you haven't already explored Sibu's seven-storey **Chinese Pagoda** near the banks of the Rajang, take a quick look at this striking modern landmark before heading for the upriver express jetty. As timetables are frequently changed, check the departure time of boats for Kapit in advance; try to book on one of the Husqvarna Express boats, the most modern and comfortable. Take a boat going directly to Kapit, rather than one stopping at Song and Kanowit on the way.

The Rajang, at 563km (350 miles) the longest river in Malaysia, is one of Sarawak's major highways, with express boats, tugs, timber barges, longboats and even the occasional dugout canoe all

Riding the rapids

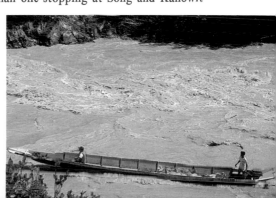

plying its muddy waters. Iban longhouses can be found along the Rajang and on the banks of its many tributaries, with several older, more traditional longhouses up the Katibas river, near Song. This is where to go if you want to strike out on your own.

Kapit, roughly 2½ hours from Sibu, is the last major administrative post along the Rajang. Thanks to newly created timber wealth, Kapit has grown into a busy little centre with a couple of fast-food joints and the inevitable karaoke in several Chinese restaurants, yet it still retains some of its frontier flavour. Express boats from upriver crowd the busy Kapit jetty as men unload carcasses of wild boar, deer and other more exotic wildlife destined for the market. Kayan and Kenyah women (many of the older ones with tattooed hands and arms and elongated ear lobes) buy and sell or enjoy a break in the local coffee shops, rubbing shoulders with the dominant Iban, as well as Melanau and Chinese.

Kapit's **open market** is full of intriguing jungle produce and a fascinating mixture of people. If you're interested in old handicrafts, try Lai Lai Handicraft & Antique Co, on the ground floor of the four-storey modern shop-houses tucked back against the hillside behind the Gelanggang Kenyalang market. The prices aren't nec-

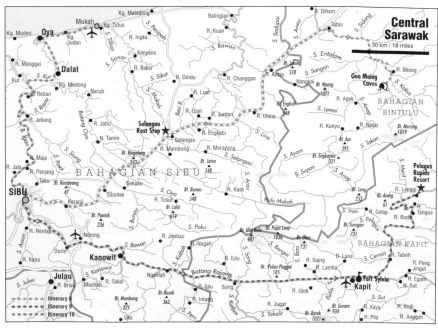

essarily cheaper than in Kuching, but you may find some fine old Iban textiles among the bric-a-brac.

Just upriver from the jetty is the white-painted **Fort Sylvia**, built in 1875 by Charles Brooke to prevent the Iban from moving upriver and clashing with the Kayan, Kenyah and other Orang Ulu. The small but interesting museum currently located in the **Dewan Suarah** (Civic Centre) near the hospital is due to move into this quaint wooden fort topped by ironwood shingles. Look on the outside wall for a plaque indicating the level reached by the Rajang during a massive flood. In front of the fort is a stone placed in 1994 to commemorate 70 years of peace between the Iban and Orang Ulu, who held a massive Peace Making Ceremony on the site in November 1924.

Iban at Rumah George

You should already have made your booking with the **Pelagus Rapids Resort** (*see page 82*), which will arrange for your 45-minute speedboat transfer from Kapit. The resort is a delightfully unpretentious place set in a rainforest reserve along the Rajang. Staying in a genuine longhouse is a wonderful experience, but at times it's great to have a little luxury and privacy and this is one of the nicest places in Sarawak to indulge yourself.

Immediately upriver from the resort is the first of the seven dangerous rapids which formed the traditional natural boundary between the Iban and the upriver Kayan, Kenyah and other Orang Ulu. The Pelagus Rapids Resort, an adaptation of a traditional Iban longhouse designed by notable Kuching architect Edric Ong, is built entirely of native timber. Check out the stunning entrance doors, carved by Kenyah artist Tusau Padan.

You'll want to relax after a long day's travel, maybe just by sitting on your balcony watching the river, swimming in the pool or playing a game of darts. Next morning, if you haven't already checked out the **information centre**, do so; it's one of the best in Sarawak. Well primed with information about the environment, take a walk along one of the forest trails with a guide.

I recommend taking a tour downriver by longboat to **Rumah George**, an Iban longhouse tucked away on a tributary of the Rajang. Despite its relative modernity and Western name, Rumah George is full of women weaving magnificent traditional fabrics at their back-strap looms. You'll be greeted with the traditional *miring* ceremony, and after a few glasses of *tuak* you won't feel self-conscious about getting up and dancing. You'll be treated to lunch (probably rice with wild ferns and other jungle vegetables, plus some wild boar or chicken), and then it's time for a short walk. However, if you want to pause and take forty winks on the communal verandah to diminish

Canoeing through the rainforest

the effects of your *tuak*, that will be considered perfectly natural.

It's surprisingly easy to reach the lovely **waterfall** near Rumah George. Just cross the river, follow the trail for five minutes and there you are, gazing in delight at a crystal-clear cascade splashing into a surprisingly cool pool surrounded by rainforest.

After another peaceful night at the Pelagus Rapids resort, you might like to try your hand at fishing on the Rajang, or following the trail upriver for a good view of the first rapids.

9. Orang Ulu Longhouse and Caves

This two-night trip takes you to a Punan Bah longhouse along the Kakus river, one of the most striking traditional longhouses still standing in Sarawak. Further upriver, at Gua Maing, valuable birds' nests are gathered in an outcrop of limestone caves reached via beautiful rainforest.

As Sarawak's old longhouses are constantly being replaced by modern versions, it becomes increasingly difficult to find massive old wooden structures full of charm and character, with a huge cool verandah rather than a poky, cement-floored apology for a *ruai*. **Rumah Bilong** is one of my favourite Sarawak longhouses and is remarkably accessible, being only 2 hours by boat from **Tatau**, a village easily reached by bus from Sibu or Bintulu.

If you're coming from Sibu, take an express bus towards Bintulu and ask to be let off at Pekan Tatau, or take the regular (but slower) Sibu–Tatau bus which will take about 2½ hours, including a pause at Selangau (one of Sarawak's many rest stops). A mini-bus or regular scheduled bus heading south from Bintulu takes about an hour to reach Tatau.

Tatau is a divided town. The new Pekan Tatau is an unlovely collection of coffee shops and general

Waiting for an express boat

stores, with upriver express boats (owned by several of the coffee-shop proprietors in this new complex) leaving from just in front of the Shell station. The romantic old **Tatau Bazaar** (the settlement was established in 1906), about 10 minutes' walk upriver, is losing business to the newer shops frequented by those gathering to catch an express boat close by. For a feeling of bygone Sarawak, visit the old bazaar with its tidy wooden shops opening onto a boardwalk, decorated with plants and benches for folk to sit and pass the time of day. Watch out for women sitting at a table in many of the shop fronts, painstakingly picking out feathers and other impurities from soaked birds' nests which have come from the Gua Maing caves upriver.

The non-air-conditioned express boat for Lana will let you off at **Rumah Bilong** (which, on old maps, may still be referred to as Rumah Keseng); boats currently depart at 9am, 12.30pm and 1.30pm, but check at the jetty as soon as you get off your bus. The boats load up with sacks of rice, sugar, cement, LPG bottles and other essentials for the logging camps further upriver.

Watch out from the right side of the express boat as you head upriver; after about half an hour, you'll see five carved wooden funerary poles, or *keltrieng*, in which the bones of departed aristocrats were placed. The Kajang, an Orang Ulu group comprising the Punan Bah, Sekapan, Kejaman and Lahanan people, were famed for erecting these magnificent structures, carved from *belian* or iron-wood. You'll catch only a glimpse as the express boat whizzes by, but you can look more closely at *kelirieng* in the grounds of Kuching's Sarawak Museum.

At Rumah Bilong

After about two hours, you'll reach Rumah Bilong. As you climb up from the river towards the headman's quarters in the centre of the huge longhouse, you'll see an important traditional structure, a *salong*, or storage house for bones of the departed, with Chinese porcelain plates and bowls stuck into the timber as decoration. The *salong* is actually a Kayan and Kenyah tradition adopted by the Punan Bah and other Kajang groups when a ban on secondary burial made it no longer possible to erect the *kelirieng* (the fact that tradition demanded two slaves be crushed to death beneath the *kelirieng* as it was raised may also have had something to do with its demise).

When you climb the notched log onto the verandah of the longhouse, ask to see the headman's daughter, Ado, or her husband, Bugang Sati. They will probably invite you to stay in their modern house connected to the back of their traditional longhouse quarters, or arrange for you to stay with another family. Be sure to offer to pay for your lodging, and bring gifts such as fresh fruit, magazines, cigarettes and sweets.

The main longhouse here is like an entire village, with 64 'doors' or family quarters opening off the huge verandah, which is so long that it takes a definite curve somewhere along the way. A carved wooden pillar outside the headman's quarters measures more than 2m (7ft) in circumference and is thought to be well over a century old. In the past, when longhouses were moved to a more fertile location, the inhabitants transported the pillars and belian roof tiles with them. As well as the main longhouse, there is an adjacent, smaller, more modern, 34-door longhouse.

It's easy to spend the rest of the day exploring Rumah Bilong and its environs, chatting with the people, watching the women weaving and the younger children tumbling with the puppies. The Punan Bah, like many of the other Orang Ulu, traditionally had a stratified society. Almost all the residents of Rumah Bilong have converted to Christianity and it is difficult to assess how many of their traditional beliefs and customs still remain.

Punan Bah woman

Ask Bugang to take you upriver the next day to **Gua Maing**, the caves where his ancestors were given rights to the birds' nests by Rajah Charles Brooke way back in 1913 (he may even show you the original title deed). Don't forget you'll need to pay for petrol; check in advance what the charge will be – remember, private river travel is always expensive in Sarawak.

The trip by longboat to Gua Maing is magnificent once you leave the muddy Kakus and start heading along ever-smaller streams through virgin rainforest. With any luck, you'll see brilliant broadbills, kingfishers, herons and perhaps even a scarlet trogon as you push through the dense vegetation. After about 1½ hours, you'll reach a cleared area in front of the caves, where quarters for the birds'-nest collectors and some accommodation intended for visitors have been erected. (Bugang may offer you the chance to stay here, but once you've explored the caves, there's not a lot going on at Gua Maing.)

The limestone outcrop riddled with caves where swiftlets build their edible nests is only 200–300m (650–980ft) high, and has a river running through. It's of a manageable size and pleasant to explore. If you're fortunate, you may see the collectors, many of them young Indonesians, scaling poles and ladders to scrape the birds' nests off the cave walls and roof.

Mukah fishing fleet

10. Mellow Out in Mukah

Explore the villages around Mukah, perhaps the prettiest coastal town in Sarawak and rarely visited by tourists. Here in the heartland of the Melanau, you can see sago being processed in the traditional way, feast on *umai*, the excellent raw fish salad, paddle up a river through the swamp forest or cycle along a beach at sunset.

The easiest way to reach **Mukah** is to fly from Kuching or Sibu. Alternatively, take a direct bus from Sibu, or get off a Bintulu–Sibu bus at Selangau and transfer to a local one heading for Mukah. Either way, you'll have about an hour of bumping along an un-surfaced road as you head for the coast. You'll pass large oil palm plantations and some of the neatest modern longhouses you'll en-counter in Sarawak before coming to the coast, where the Iban population gives way to the Melanau.

The Melanau, one of the original tribes of Sarawak, once lived along the Rajang river as far up as Kapit, but were gradually forced down to coastal areas by the Iban, Kayan and Kenyah, who migrated from Kalimantan. Almost half the Melanau are now Muslim; the rest either remain pagan or have converted to Christianity. They no longer live in big communal houses (have a look at the Melanau High House at the Sarawak Cultural Village) but have adopted the architecture, lifestyle and dress of the Malays. Like many others who adopted Islam, Muslim Melanau once referred to themselves as Malay. Recently, however, a sense of individuality has resulted in their proudly declaring themselves Melanau (including the Chief Minister, Tan Sri Abdul Taib Mahmud).

As you approach Mukah, you'll see the long, shallow coastline, where the beaches are good for strolling and watching the sunset, but not, alas, for swimming. Mukah spreads on both sides of the Mukah river, about a 1km (½ mile) in from the coast, and you'll soon appreciate how important both the river and sea are to local life. The river road is lined by old Chinese shop houses, with the town's best hotel, the **King Ing**, facing a Chinese temple at one end, and the mar-ket set next to a distinctive bus stop with a roof painted to look like a *terendak*, the typical Melanau hat, at the other.

It is worth paying a visit to the **District Office**, where you may be able to rent a bicycle and pose any queries you might have to the officer responsible for tourism. I've always found the staff of Sarawak's District Offices (responsible for government administration outside major centres) extremely helpful and friendly, and Mukah is no exception.

The District Office should also be able to advise you of the date (generally late March/early April) of the **Pesta Kaul**, the festival which is basically a blessing for fishermen at the end of the northeast monsoon, marking the start of the new fishing season, as well as a ritual to get rid of any illness and increase the yield of the sago trees. The 'official' Pesta Kaul, held in an open area not far from the airport, incorporates a Muslim blessing and features a large traditional wooden swing. A non-Muslim (and more traditional) Pesta Kaul is held by some of the villagers of Kampung Tellian Ulu, as well as in Oya.

The focus of life in Mukah is the **market**, where groups of men chat and smoke as they await the arrival of the fishing boats at around 9am, and again at about 4pm. The catch (often strung together with a strip of rattan) scarcely has time to lie on the sheet of plastic spread on the ground under a tree before it's snapped up and taken home. Some of the fish is destined for *umai*; look for the couple at the edge of the market who fillet and shred the fish and then sell it for making this Melanau speciality. If you want to taste the prepared dish, ask them to mix it for you on the spot.

The nicest place to enjoy *umai* and other fabulous fresh seafood for either lunch or dinner is the **Nibong House Seafood Restaurant** in Jalan Orang Kaya Setiaraja. Open-sided and surrounded by a lovely garden, the restaurant offers food as delightful as the setting. There is a **mini-museum** of Melanau culture on the top floor of the **Dewan Suarah**, or Civic Centre, opposite the restaurant; it's worth going up for a look at the various handicrafts and artefacts (open daily, 8am–4.15pm).

When you've explored the town, it's time for **Kampung Tellian Ulu**, just 7km (4 miles) from Mukah. You can either take a mini-bus, rent a bicycle or hire a taxi (ask the driver to wait or return

Taking a slow boat

A carved ritual figure

to collect you). There are actually three Tellian villages, almost running into each other; the furthest from town (**Tellian Ulu**) is opposite a Christian cemetery. This collection of wooden houses perched on either side of the inky-black river (stained by the tannin leached from leaves) is linked by a wooden walkway and is ridiculously picturesque.

Ask to be taken to the house of the headman, Tua Kampung Pateran, a venerable shaman who is renowned as a traditional healer and as a carver of wooden figures used in Melanau rituals. These figures (which Tua Kampung sells for around RM60) are generally known by the Melanau of Oya and Dalat as *belum*, although here they're called *dakan*.

In this *kampung*, too, you'll be able to see sago processing. The school teacher living in Tellian Ulu speaks English and is very helpful. He will be able to arrange for someone to paddle you by canoe upriver to the plantations of sago palm, where the mature trees are felled and cut into lengths for floating down to the kampung. Sheds along the river contain rasping machines to shred the starch-laden pith of the palm, and the sago starch is washed out in hollowed logs lashed at the edge of the river. You can watch the starch being shaped into pellets, which are then toasted on a huge clay griddle over a fire, the result being crunchy balls which are an indispensable accompaniment (for the Melanau) to *umai*. You can also see the thin biscuits (*tebaloi*) made of sago starch, sugar and eggs being produced.

A sleepy Mukah backwater

If you go mid to late afternoon, when it's cooler, cycling is a great way to explore the Tellian villages, as well as the villages and the beach area west of town near the airport. Mukah is a delightful place just to hang out, visit a factory to see how the local *tebaloi* are made, have a look at a crab and tiger prawn farm, or watch the sun set into the South China Sea as you listen to the wind in the casuarina trees.

You can leave Mukah by bus or plane, but a more interesting alternative is to take the local bus to the town of **Dalat**. Here, you should be able to take a boat which winds along a channel cut through the swamp forest to the village of **Kut**, on the banks of the Batang Igan, a larger river which will take you down to Sibu. The boats cannot depart at extreme low tide, but if you happen to be unlucky, you can always stay the night in the government resthouse or in a lodging house in Dalat.

Miri & The Northeast

Miri, Sarawak's third biggest town, is the jumping-off point for Gunung Mulu National Park, the Kelabit Highlands, longhouses up the Baram river, the small Lambir Hills National Park and the famous Niah Caves. Miri can be reached by air from the major centres of Kuching, Sibu and Bintulu, and also by express bus from these three towns. If you are coming from the north, you can fly or take a bus from Bandar Seri Begawan in Brunei, or fly directly from Kota Kinabalu in Sabah.

11. Miri and Niah Caves

Start early for a quick look at Miri's lively native market before heading down to the Niah Caves, Borneo's most important archaeological site where birds' nests are still gathered. Spend the night surrounded by forest in the national park accommodation, returning to Miri the following day.

Miri, 'Queen of the North', became a boom town after the discovery of oil in 1910. Although the petroleum industry has been reduced in importance, palm oil and the timber industry ensure Miri is still a busy centre.

Edible flowers

Unless it's holiday season or the weekend (best avoided if you're seeking serenity), you shouldn't have difficulty booking accommodation on arrival at **Niah National Park**. To make sure, book in advance at the nearest Visitors' Information Centre (*see page 86*). Have an early breakfast at one of the many coffee shops around Miri and then head for the **Tamu Muhibbah**, the fascinating produce market opposite the Miri Visitors' Information Centre. There are two buildings here, the most interesting being the one at the back

Selling local produce

where tattooed Orang Ulu women, some with elongated earlobes, rub shoulders with Iban and Malay women selling a bewildering range of jungle produce: wild ferns, heart of palm, Bario's famous rice, wriggling sago grubs (eaten after they're briefly dipped in boiling water), smoked dried fish, bamboo tubes for steaming chicken to make *pansuh*, dried loofahs, palm sugar, exotic jungle fruits – it's hard to decide which is more intriguing, the produce or the sellers.

Opposite the market and next to the Visitors' Information Centre, there is a local bus and taxi station where you can pick up a taxi to the **Niah Caves**. To charter the cab right to the park entrance will cost RM80; if you share with three other passengers, the fare to the town of Batu Niah is RM15 per head, with another RM5 on to the park. Buses operated by Syarikat Bas Suria run from Miri (10 buses daily) or Bintulu (8 buses daily). From Miri, the fare to Batu Niah is currently RM8.50; pick up the Batu Niah bus at the stop opposite the Visitors' Information Centre, or take a shuttle bus (No 4) from the local bus/taxi station to the long distance bus station about 6km (4 miles) north of town. The early buses leave this station at 6.45am, 7.30am, 8.30am and 9.30am, arriving at the town stop around 10 minutes later.

The road to Batu Niah follows the main highway for about 1½ hours, passing **Lambir Hills National Park** 30km (19 miles) out of Miri; this park is renowned for the diversity of its forest, its treetop tower and waterfalls. You'll see plenty of oil palm plantations and modern Iban longhouses along the road until you reach the Batu Niah turnoff. It's about another 10–15 minutes to this village, which is dominated by the Chinese who originally came here to trade in birds' nests and to plant pepper along the rich river flats.

If you've come by bus, I recommend saving time and paying RM10 for a taxi from Batu Niah to Niah National Park 12km (7½ miles) by road. Stock up on fresh fruit in town if you want to supplement your meals at the park's canteen, and if you'd like beer (not available at the park), buy it here to keep in the fridge in your hostel or chalet. If you don't mind a 40-minute walk, head from

The Great Cave at Niah

the bus stop in Batu Niah – keeping the limestone outcrop of Gunung Subis on your right – past the Batu Niah Billiard Parlour, until you see the small National Park sign. Turn left along this gravel road, past a large school on your right and a gaudy Chinese temple on your left. The 2km (1 mile) trail, which is mostly shaded, passes by some rather scruffy Iban houses and continues along the riverside to the park's side entrance.

Niah National Park's hostels are the most luxurious in Sarawak. Each spacious room has four beds rather than double bunks, and its own bathroom with a hot shower. Each hostel has a fridge, dining table and sitting room, but you must request the loan of an electric kettle and basic eating utensils.

After checking in, have a look at the **information centre**. Although some of the exhibits are (at the time of writing) in a poor state of repair, there's interesting background on the archaeology, history, geology and bird's-nest industry of the Niah Caves. Have lunch at the park canteen then, equipped with torch (flashlight), water bottle and umbrella, set off for the caves. It costs 50 sen per person to chug across the small river to the start of the plank walkway leading 2.5km (1½ miles) to the entrance of the caves.

Take your time to check out the forest on both sides of the boardwalk, and don't miss the tree anchored by massive buttress roots on the left about 15 minutes along the trail. You'll hear plenty of birds, although it will take patience to spot them, and you may see squirrels and flying lizards. You might also come across Iban youths throwing a circular net, or *jala*, to catch small fish and even sizeable freshwater prawns in the stream along the trail. When you pass an impromptu stall selling cold drinks and souvenirs on the right of the boardwalk, you'll know you've just about reached the first of the caves. A smaller boardwalk off to the left leads to **Rumah Chang**, a modern Iban longhouse where many of the birds'-nest and guano collectors live.

The guano – powdery bat and bird dung which collects on the floor of the caves – is not a particularly rich fertiliser but is valuable for preventing root disease in pepper vines. The collectors stagger along carrying 70kg (155lb) sacks of guano by a headstrap.

The entrance to the **Traders' Cave** (so called because the buyers of birds' nests used to sit here with their scales and buy directly from the collectors) is marked by a high iron gate. Although the caves are set within a national park, because of their archaeological importance they are under the control of the Museum Department and the main archaeological sites within the Great Cave and the Painted Cave are securely fenced.

The Niah Caves are remarkably important. Excavations carried out in the late 1950s produced the oldest signs of human habitation found anywhere on the island of Borneo. Pre-historic man once lived near the mouth of the Great Cave, leaving stone tools, earthenware pottery, shell ornaments and a cemetery. A skull found here is thought to be 25,000 years old.

Another reason to value the Niah Caves is the tiny swiftlets, whose edible saliva hardens to form nests in which they lay their eggs. The Chinese have always sought the nests for their medicinal value (they contain a glyco-protein believed to help the body's immune system), and the very finest, cleaned and processed nests can cost as much as US$250 for just under 38g (1oz). The nests gathered at Niah are not, however, the finest variety, but are nonetheless extremely valuable.

The swiftlets normally begin making their nests around April or May. The collectors then risk their lives scaling flimsy-looking poles and ropes to reach up to 60m (almost 200ft) into the darkest crevices of the cave roof to scrape down the nests. The persistent swiftlet builds another nest which is allowed to remain undisturbed until she lays her egg and the hatchling has flown. At this time (generally around October), the second nest is gathered.

You have to be lucky to see the collectors in action, although during most of the year you'll come across groups of men camping out in the caves near the section to which they have the rights, protecting their valuable terrain from any disturbance. The men chat, smoke and play radios inside the caves, their lights puny pinpricks in the vast inky depths.

Boardwalks take you right through the **Great Cave**, but be careful of slipping on the accumulations of guano. Unfortunately, the **Painted Cave** (reached via the rear of the Great Cave) is closed to the public to protect its fragile treasures, although you may request permission to visit by writing to the Sarawak Museum in Kuching.

The remains of wooden coffins, of the marvellous 'ship of the dead'

Bird's-nest collectors

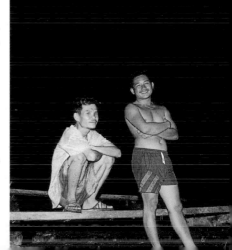

A 'ship of the dead' painting

haematite paintings, and lively renditions of human and other figures on one wall of the cave have sadly deteriorated in the past couple of decades. Thought to date back around 1,000 years, they come from a people completely different from the first cavemen of Niah, who have totally disappeared from Borneo.

If you want to view a remarkable phenomenon, wait around the mouth of the Great Cave until about 6pm, when millions of bats fly out for their nightly forage in the forest and miraculously avoid collision with the millions of swiflets returning home.

The next day, either walk back to Batu Niah along the riverside trail or, if you arranged it when you arrived, take a taxi. The early buses leave Batu Niah for Miri at 6.45am, 7.10am, 8am, 9am and 10am, the last bus being at 3.20pm. When you get back to Miri, you might like to check out a rather quaint hardware-cum-handicraft/antique store in the old part of town. At **Tiang Heng & Sons**, 51 Jalan Bendahara (the old River Road), you'll find Sarawak's best selection of Penan baskets and mats, bought directly from the Penan by the English-speaking Chinese owner. He also has other artefacts, ceramics and bric-a-brac, all at very reasonable prices.

12. Gunung Mulu National Park

Gunung Mulu is Sarawak's greatest national park, in all senses of the word. This itinerary begins with the bare minimum 2-day/1-night stay, and suggests extensions for adventure caving and trekking out of the park along a trail once used by headhunters.

When the Royal Geographical Society was invited by the Sarawak government to help in the exploration of the rainforest around **Gunung Mulu** in 1977–8, scientists were astonished to find such hidden treasures as a vast network of caves, 50m (165 ft) limestone

A rainforest blossom

pinnacles piercing the jungle, and thousands of unrecorded species of plant and animal life. Since 1985, it has been possible for ordinary visitors to make their own voyage of discovery in this magnificent 52,866-hectare (130,630-acre) national park.

You no longer need to get a permit before travelling to Mulu as this is now issued instantly when you check in at park headquarters. It is still possible to reach the park the old way, by bus and several boat rides, but you spend the entire day getting there and there's very little of interest en route, so I recommend flying. Take the earliest flight possible and enjoy the view of undisturbed forest as you fly over Brunei. Mulu's airport, just outside the park boundary, is either a boat ride, a walk or a short drive from the accommodation, which ranges from the luxurious **Royal Mulu Lodge** (*see page 81*) to a number of simple lodges run by tour operators – all located outside the park boundary – as well as hostels and chalets run by the national parks within the park (these must be booked in advance at Miri's Visitors' Information Centre). If you're coming for only one night, you don't need a tour operator as all trips within the park must be accompanied by an official park guide. However, if you're doing adventure caving or the Headhunters' Trail, I recommend making arrangements with Tropical Adventure or Borneo Adventure (*see page 87*).

Settle in, enjoy your lunch and, at around 2pm, torch (flashlight) in hand and liberally doused with mosquito repellent, go to park headquarters where you must register and pay the entrance fee and camera charge. Have a look around the **information centre** and then take the 3km (2 mile) boardwalk towards Deer Cave and Lang's

Cave (your park guide will cost you RM20). The boardwalk (which takes about 45 minutes) leads over patches of peat swamp and you'll see some massive fig trees on the way. Ask your guide to point out the *ipoh* tree where the Penan, who once roamed the forests of Mulu, collected poisonous sap for their blowpipe darts. The peat forest, incidentally, is one of eight types of forest found within the park, ranging from mixed *dipterocarp* rainforest to moss forest on the higher mountain slopes.

Once you get to **Deer Cave** (the floor of which is

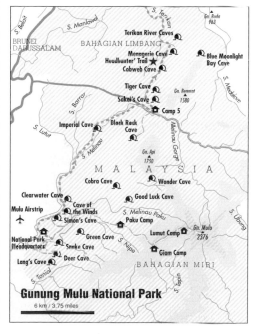

Gunung Mulu National Park
6 km / 3.75 miles

protected by a boardwalk, which has the advantage of keeping you above the muck and creepy-crawlies), your guide will probably start spouting statistics. Mulu's caves really are awesome. Deer Cave is the world's largest cave passage, **Sarawak Chamber** (which is closed to the general public) is the world's largest natural cave chamber, and **Clearwater Cave** – 107m (350ft) in length – is the longest in Southeast Asia. Forget the figures and just immerse yourself in the enormity of the place, listening for the squeaking of bats high in the nooks and crannies of the roof. You can walk through to the back where there is the totally enclosed 'Garden of Eden'.

A short walk from Deer Cave is **Lang's Cave**, the second of the four 'show caves' (those open to the public). The main attraction here is the beautiful cave formations, stalactites and stalagmites artfully lit for maximum effect. When you've explored Lang's Cave, it's time to get ready for one of Mulu's most striking phenomena: the nightly exodus of millions of bats from the cave mouths as they depart on their evening forage. Walk away from the mouth of Deer Cave, past the toilet blocks to the cleared helipad area and wait until around 6pm when, provided it's not raining, the bats will start leaving the caves. A dark stream, spiralling like smoke, eventually whirls overhead and you can hear the whirr of thousands of tiny

A Rajah Brooke Birdwing butterfly

wings. The bats keep on funnelling out of the caves for up to 20 minutes, a never-to-be-forgotten sight.

On your second day, arrange for a picnic lunch and a longboat to take you to **Wind Cave** and **Clearwater Cave**. You'll travel along the Sungai Melinau to the river bank just below Wind Cave, then it's a short, steep climb up a walkway into the cave mouth. Wander about inside the cave, where you'll feel the wind blowing through the narrowest portions. A boardwalk hugs the exterior of the cliff face, connecting Wind Cave with Clearwater Cave, only five minutes' walk away.

The entrance to Clearwater Cave is among my favourite spots in the park, with its wooden picnic shelters perched on stilts at the edge of an incredibly clear river that flows from the lower portion of the cliff face near the cave mouth. You can often see striking iridescent green and black Rajah Brooke Birdwing butterflies feeding at the damp spots near the toilet blocks, as well as a number of birds, including the Chestnut-naped Forktail. Clearwater Cave has a subterranean river which flows very fast after heavy rain. Paths and plank walks lead you into various sections of the cave, including the **King's Room** with its illuminated formations of stalactites, stalagmitos and beautiful flow stones which look like petrified waves.

When you've finished exploring the cave, it's time for a swim in the cool Clearwater river, and then for your picnic lunch. If you're doing the 'minimum Mulu', you'll need to think about heading back to catch the late afternoon flight to Miri.

If you're doing the Headhunters' Trail, you'll continue upriver to **Kuala Berar**, where you trek for 2–3 hours through the forest to Camp 5 to spend the night in a basic jungle shelter. Most tour operators offer you a chance to climb to the **Pinnacles** the next day, a very strenuous one-day trip which takes you up (and up) through the moss forest to a spot where you can gaze down on these much-photographed limestone needles. At the risk of sounding unadventurous, I'd recommend skipping the trip to the Pinnacles and, instead, setting off on the 11-km (7-mile) trek from Camp 5 to Kuala Terikan.

Equipped for trekking

Part of this trail follows the route used by Kayan warriors on their way down to attack Muruts and Chinese pepper farmers along the Limbang river during the bad old headhunting days. They had to haul their longboats along a 4 m (13 ft) wide trail laid with poles for about 3 km (2 miles) through the jungle, before paddling down the Terikan river. You won't have to haul a boat, however, and your main challenge – if the vegetation is wet – will be the leeches. Once you get to the Terikan, it'll be a 2-hour boat ride to **Rumah Balasong**, an Iban longhouse, where you'll spend the night before going by boat to Nanga Medamit and then taking a bus down to Limbang.

If you decide to stay longer in Mulu before flying back to Miri, you can spend a day relaxing, birdwatching, paddling a kayak on the River Benarat or adventure caving. For the latter, you'll be provided with a caving helmet, but bring your own light gloves, water bottle and shoes with a good grip.

It's not everyone's idea of a great way to spend a day, ploughing about in mud and bat dung in the pitch darkness, and if you aren't physically fit, adventurous and untroubled by claustrophobia, you shouldn't even consider it.

If you have time to do only one trek in Sarawak, I'd recommend this 4-day itinerary, which takes you from the fertile rice-growing plateau of Bario through Kelabit settlements and virgin rainforest to Ba Kelalan. See Borneo at its most beautiful and learn the secrets of the forest from your Kelabit guide.

*—This trek is through a very remote region, so requires a certain amount of advance planning, including early booking of your air ticket from Miri to **Bario**, and from Ba Kelalan via Lawas back to Miri. Be aware that flights are frequently cancelled owing to bad weather, so try to leave a few days at the end of the trip before you have to leave Sarawak.—*

The trip is moderately demanding, so make sure you're fit before setting off. It is essential to have a guide; either contact a tour operator who will arrange everything from air tickets to food to guides (I recommend Tropical Adventure, *see page 87*), or fly to Bario and ask for a freelance guide there. Better still, write in advance

to one of the guides listed on page 87. Guides and porters currently charge RM60 a day, and you will be expected to pay for one extra day for their return trip from Ba Kelalan to Bario. I heartily recommend hiring a porter.

If you use a freelance guide, you will need to supply most of your own food.

Rice-growing on the Bario plateau

Unless you are content with rice three times a day, bring sachets of instant potato, dried soups and freeze-dried food from home. Muesli, powdered milk, instant noodles, sugar, instant coffee, biscuits, dried fruit, nuts and snacks can be found at Parkson Grand supermarket in Miri's Bintang Plaza. Your guide should be able to provide Bario's famous rice, wild jungle vegetables, wild boar and perhaps some fish.

Your trip begins with a flight on the MAS Rural Air Service Twin Otter jet from Miri to Bario − 1,128m (3,700ft) above sea level. This is the only way to get there unless you walk in from Ba Kelalan. Keep your baggage light as both you and your bags will be weighed and you may have to pay an excess baggage fee. Try to get a seat on the left side of the plane so you can look down on the limestone mountains of **Gunung Mulu National Park** en route. You may spot the mouth of Deer Cave, and later see the twin peaks of Batu Lawi − 2,043m (6,700ft) thrusting up through the jungle.

Depending on the time of the year, the rice fields of the Bario

Wrapping up cooked rice

plateau will be lush green or rich gold, with the corrugated iron roofs of its nine scattered settlements glinting in the sun. Try to avoid visiting in November and December, when it rains most frequently, increasing the notorious leech population along the trails. The harvest season of February to March is usually dry, while the rest of the year you will just have to pray that the weather god is smiling on you.

The Kelabit people living in the high plateau sprawling across northeastern Sarawak and Indonesian Kalimantan are renowned for their sophisticated wet-rice culture and produce several varieties of excellent, organically grown rice. Many Kelabit people still live in longhouses, but as the entire community is now evangelical Christian on both sides of the border, they no longer indulge in drinking rice wine or any other kind of alcohol (you won't even get a beer up here; if you bring your own supplies, please be discreet). The Kelabit are as warmly welcoming as any of Sarawak's people, and have a great knowledge of and respect for the virgin forest.

During the Japanese Occupation of World War II, a group of Allied Armed Forces, including the colourful Tom Harrisson (*see* 'Recommended Reading', *page 88*) parachuted into Bario to organise resistance. Outside attention was again focused on the area during Indonesia's confrontation with Malaysia in 1963, and once more in the 1970s, when communist terrorist stragglers hid out in the surrounding jungle.

When you arrive in Bario (which will be at around 10 or 11am), trek with your guide to the small shopping area opposite Tarawes guesthouse and near the fancy blue-roofed guesthouse (due to open 1998). Check in to your accommodation or, if your guide intends taking you to his longhouse, leave your bag in one of the market shops. Here you can have a quick bite before trekking to the **Bario Asal longhouse**, on the original site of the settlement.

Unlike other Sarawak longhouses, the communal area here is the kitchen and eating area – which is very sensible, as this is where the warm cooking fires are located. The evenings and mornings are surprisingly cool up in the highlands, which makes trekking a delight owing to the lack of humidity.

The next day, it's a 4–5-hour trek to the beautifully situated village of **Pa Lungan**. Between Bario and the first village en route, **Pa Ukat** (about an hour along a wide trail), you'll see lots of pitcher plants, rhododendrons and lovely white and purple ground orchids. As there's no forest cover, it can be very hot, so remember to bring an umbrella on this trip as well as a hat. About an hour out of Pa Ukat, you will see enigmatic faces carved into a large rock (**Batu Narit**) on the right of the trail, one of several megaliths found in the Bario region. It will take another 2–3 hours' easy trekking over gentle hills to reach Pa Lungan, where, with luck, you'll feast on wild boar at night.

On the third day, the trail winds through magnificent virgin forest for the 5–6 hour trek to **Long Rapung**. After the first couple of hours, you climb a steep hill and follow the ridge for some distance before going down an even steeper, slippery trail. Ask your guide to show you the site (on the right of the trail about half an hour before you reach Long Rapung) where *Rafflesia priceii* grows; if you're lucky enough to be here at the right time, you may see the world's largest flower in full bloom.

Long Rapung was the site of a longhouse whose inhabitants had to be resettled during the 1963 confrontation, leaving behind their fruit trees (you can still see tamarillos and pomelos, as well as the remains of their coffee plants). The setting is idyllic: giant bamboo groves, a clear, cool stream where you can fish and enjoy a bath, and a solid wooden shelter built by the locals who frequently

A graceful rock carving

stop here en route for Indonesia. After your busy day, you're sure to sleep soundly at night (provided you remembered your mosquito coils and repellent).

You'll start early on the fourth day, the most demanding of the trip. It will take 8–10 hours to reach **Ba Kelalan**, depending on your fitness and how long you pause at the Indonesian army checkpoint. You'll perhaps set off to the musical calls of gibbons, although you're unlikely to see wild animals, and even the birds, which you hear constantly, tend to be difficult to spot. Before you get too tired, keep your eyes open for the small details that make the rainforest so fascinating: bright red ginger flowers pushing straight up from the earth; dozens of fungi in all colours; a giant tree oozing damar resin or a spray of vivid orchids. You'll cross many streams, using logs which will test your sense of balance.

The border with Indonesia is on a ridge, and you keep on trekking down through forest and along a lush valley filled with paddy fields and water buffalo. The somewhat scruffy village of **Pa Rupai** is quickly passed, and after a slog along level ground, crossing countless bamboo stiles and perhaps feasting on wild raspberries, you'll come to **Long Medang**. The trail starts uphill and passes an Indonesian army checkpoint, where you'll be obliged to show your passport. If you're lucky (and offer snacks and cigarettes on arrival), the Indonesians may send you on your way with a smile. You may, however, be forced to pay bribes (RM100 per head for the travellers who passed about a month before I did) – there's nothing you can do about it, as you're passing through Indonesia 'unofficially' without a visa.

After re-crossing the border, there's one more very steep descent to do before reaching a grassy valley where water buffalo are quarantined, then you walk through more idyllic surroundings, replete with streams and rice paddies, before you reach the Malaysian army

checkpoint. A passport check, a few questions and smiles, and you're on your way, wondering just how much longer it takes to reach **Buduk Nur**, the village nestled next to Ba Kelalan airstrip. It's a wonderful surprise to turn a corner just a few minutes later and see the cluster of houses which signals civilisation.

Spend the night here and enjoy a well-deserved rest before catching the flight next morning to Lawas, with a connection on down to Miri.

A wild ginger flower

Shopping

If you love handicrafts, curios and antiques, you'll go wild in Kuching, where the concentration of craft shops along Main Bazaar can keep you occupied for hours. In other parts of Sarawak, you will find a limited selection of curios in hotel shops and in one or two stores (mentioned in the relevant itineraries). Longhouses accustomed to receiving groups of visitors often display handwoven fabric, baskets, mats and beadwork for sale. You may be able to

Baskets come in all shapes and sizes

purchase old Iban *pua kumbu* (ceremonial blankets), antique Orang Ulu beads or a fine baby carrier. But don't try too hard to persuade longhouse people to part with their precious heirlooms; you can always buy items people really want to sell back in Kuching. Bargaining is expected, everywhere from the longhouse to the city craft shops; even in the classiest hotel shops you may be able to get a discount, especially if buying more than one or two items. Dealers along Main Bazaar are accustomed to packing and shipping goods overseas, and will accept major credit cards.

Antiques

Everything from Chinese ceramic jars to carved wooden figures and gold ornaments on chains can be found in Main Bazaar's shops. Be sure to check it's a genuine antique if you're asked to pay antique prices. Three shops I recommend, where the dealers are knowledgeable and have a reputation for honesty, are:

Arts of Asia, 68 Main Bazaar, which has an enviable collection of handicrafts and furniture. Genuine antique furniture is increasingly hard to find, but owner Jimmy Teo has a range of modern copies of colonial furniture made in Java.

Atelier Gallery, 104 Main Bazaar, the closest antique shop to the Chinese temple, and the most beautifully arranged; look at the courtyard garden and go upstairs to see how various antiques, reproduction

An ornate baby carrier

furniture and other pieces can be displayed to best advantage. Tasteful items from all over Asia.

Nelson's Gallery, 84 Main Bazaar (no sign, next to Sin Wah Hui coffee shop). Proprietor Nelson Tan is the doyen of Kuching's antique dealers and has some fantastic treasures hidden away. If you're a serious collector, ask to see him personally. Sister Angie runs the front of the shop with great charm, while brother John manages the neighbouring shop at 62 Main Bazaar.

Baby Carriers

Sometimes made of simple carved wood (generally from Kalimantan), sometimes beautifully decorated with coins, bear's claws and intricate beadwork designs, baby carriers are precious items that can easily cost RM1,000 or more.

Basket Ware

Entire books have been written on the basket ware produced by different ethnic groups in Sarawak. **Main Bazaar** in Kuching and the stores near the **Sibu express boat wharf** are good places to see a range of baskets, which are one of Sarawak's best buys. For the best selection of Penan baskets and mats in Sarawak, try **Tiang Heng & Sons**, 51 Jalan Bendahara, Miri, which has a range of basket ware, antiques and handicrafts mixed up with normal hardware supplies.

Beads and Beadwork

Antique beads are highly prized by many of Sarawak's people, especially the Orang Ulu. They can be bought by the strand and are sometimes sold singly in the shops along **Main Bazaar**. Buy a few and create your own earrings if you can't afford an entire necklace.

Birds' Nests

Believed by the Chinese to have medicinal properties, these are gathered and processed in Sarawak so are cheaper here than in many other cities. Ask Cynthia Phua at **Sin Hock Thai** on Main Bazaar to show you the range of birds' nests and other medicinal products she has on sale.

Books

The Sarawak Museum Shop has one of the best selections of books in Sarawak, and they are clearly displayed so you can see what's in stock. **Mohamed Yahia** in the Holiday Inn and the basement of Sarawak Plaza in Kuching also has a good selection. **The Curio Shoppe** in the Hilton, run by the same organisation as the museum

Iban ikat textiles are among the finest in the world

shop, has a good range of Borneo books as well as magazines and novels. Another option is **Times Books** in Riverside Complex. In Miri, try the gift shops in the **Holiday Inn** and **Rihga Royal**, or the Book Centre on the first floor of **Wisma Pelita Tunku**. To order books in advance, contact **Borneo Books Services**, PO Box 13908, 88845 Kota Kinabalu, Sabah, Malaysia; Fax: 60-88-213963; e-mail: bbooks@tm.netmy. It has over 500 books in stock and will ship anywhere in the world.

Carvings

Wood, horn, bone and bamboo are all carved by different ethnic groups in Sarawak and Kalimantan to create utilitarian items and ritual objects. Check out the shops in **Main Bazaar**.

Clothing

Although the department stores and hotel shops offer a range of clothing, the best place to find inexpensive T-shirts and casual items such as shorts and sun visors is along **Main Bazaar**.

Jewellery

Amber, recently discovered near Kapit, is fashioned into jewellery and sold at the Hilton gift shop, **Galeri M**, by Margaret Tan. She also has some fine silver jewellery incorporating Sarawakian motifs (but made in Bali).

Mats

Although old rattan mats, which are wonderfully soft yet strong, can sometimes be found, most of the stores along **Main Bazaar** sell new mats made from split rattan, or *pandanus*.

A carved stool

Paintings

Art works by some of Sarawak's best-known artists are frequently displayed in the lobby of the Hilton Hotel and sold at the **Galeri M** gift shop.

Pepper

Pick a peck of (un)pickled peppers at any of the souvenir stores along Main Bazaar, or in the supermarkets. Sarawak's black and white peppercorns are among the world's best. You can also find the Saraspice brand of prepared pepper sauces and *sambals*, which are excellent.

Pottery

Chinese potters incorporate traditional motifs into a range of items including vases and lampstands. A limited selection, to whet the appetite, can be found in the curio shops of **Main Bazaar**. If you want to see the whole range, take a taxi or an STC bus (No 3, 3A, 9 or 9B) from the post office to Jalan Penrissen and ask to get off at **Ng Hua Seng Pottery**.

Textiles

Handwoven Iban textiles are some of the finest *ikat* fabrics in the world. Modern blanket-sized pieces (*pua kumbu*) and smaller items are widely available along **Main Bazaar**, but if you are a serious collector the finer thread and the vegetable dyes of the older textiles make them well worth the higher price. **Fabriko**, at 56 Main Bazaar, sells a range of fabrics and clothing incorporating traditional motifs, as well as old and new Iban textiles.

A market vendor

Markets

The **Sunday Market**, which takes place just off Jalan Satok, in Kuching, starts on Saturday afternoon and runs into Sunday morning. It's worth visiting, both for the atmosphere and for the chance of finding something absolutely irresistible that you didn't know you needed. The night markets which spring up along the pavements in most sizeable towns each evening are fun for browsing and a good place to get cheap local food, as well as cassettes of Malay and Canto-pop music – very 'ethnic' and inexpensive. Native markets, or *tamu* (housed separately from the general markets), are fascinating places to see local produce, buy fruits and pick up cheap, home-grown dried gourds or loofahs. The market vendors (mostly women) are usually as photogenic as their produce.

Eating Out

Whatever you do, don't miss the opportunity of enjoying some of Sarawak's favourite dishes. Top of the list is Sarawak or Kuching *laksa*, always sold as a breakfast dish, a satisfying noodle soup of chicken stock enriched with spicy coconut milk, combined with bean sprouts, shredded omelette, chicken and prawns, garnished with a sprig of fresh coriander and served with a chilli and lime condiment, or *sambal*. Two types of fern plucked from the jungle, *paku* and the much finer *midin*, are excellent, especially when cooked with chilli *sambal*. *Umai*, a Melanau speciality, combines raw fish with lime juice, chillies and other tangy seasonings, and is traditionally served with deep-fried sago balls. Baked over a fire in a bamboo tube, *pansuh* is a longhouse favourite containing either chicken or pork. If you're upriver, ask in coffee shops or restaurants if they have wild deer (*payau*) or wild boar (*babi hutan*).

Edible jungle ferns

Sarawak is a great place to eat, with a wide range of food available at remarkably low prices. You'll get all the usual Malaysian favourites here – spicy Malay, Indian vegetarian cuisine, robust Indian Muslim food, all kinds of mouthwatering Chinese cuisine – as well as Western fast food, standard international cuisine (in the hotels), Thai, Korean and Japanese, plus a number of distinctive local dishes. The seafood is particularly good and the lush tropical fruit irresistible.

Do your taste buds (and pocket) a favour and venture outside your hotel. Standards of hygiene are good and you can eat almost anywhere with confidence. Apart from speciality restaurants, you'll find coffee shops all over Sarawak, selling a range of dishes as well as coffee, tea and other drinks: you may find one offering *satay*, another *laksa*, yet another selling a range of ready-cooked dishes. Coffee shops are usually open, fan-cooled and informal places.

Food centres with a clustering of speciality food stalls can be found in almost every town in Sarawak, and range from the big new air-conditioned A La Carte Food Court in Kuching to the excellent open-air Malay stalls next to Brooke Inn in Miri.

Some personal favourites in the major towns are listed below; other special dishes or interesting places to eat are mentioned in the various itineraries.

Kuching
Seafood

Umai, a Melanau speciality

BENSON'S SEAFOOD
49 Jalan Abell

Tucked away near the river, this highly regarded and informal seafood restaurant is best reached by walking between the Holiday Inn and Sarawak Plaza, continuing past a brightly lit seafood restaurant on the right with tables set out by the river, then going through the gap in the corrugated iron fence: Benson's is on your right. A range of fresh seafood and vegetables is set out on ice for you to choose from; request how you'd like it cooked (steamed, fried with chilli, butter-fried, etc) or ask the Captain for his recommendations. Don't miss the soupy fried Foochow noodles here; hard to find better anywhere in Sarawak. If they have bamboo clams (*ambal*), ask for them fried with garlic. Open for dinner only.

SEE GOOD
Wisma Si Kiong, Bukit Mata

Located behind the Malaysia Airlines building, this informal seafood restaurant sprawls over several levels both inside and out. Excellent range of fresh seafood, cooked in a gutsy style; ask owners Mr and Mrs Kong to recommend dishes for you. Good value and even better food. Open every evening, except the fourth and 18th day of each month.

Mixed

A LA CARTE FOOD COURT
Leboh Temple/Leboh Wayang

This air-conditioned food centre in the basement of a new multi-storey carpark (just off Main Bazaar near the Tua Peh Kong temple) houses several of the famous stalls that used to be near the old Rex Cinema. Spacious, clean and cool (especially welcome at midday), with attendants running around in aprons and bright yellow sun visors, this offers a range of local food plus Western dishes. Wander around and order what looks good.

THOMPSON'S CORNER
Corner of Jalan Nanas and Jalan Satok

A short taxi or bus ride from the Waterfront, this is one of Kuching's most popular food centres, with *laksa*, Chinese noodles, Indian food and just about anything else you might fancy.

TOPSPOT FOOD COURT
Jalan Mata Kuching

A range of Malay, Chinese and Western food sold each evening in the unlikely setting of the landscaped roof of a multi-storey car park. Lots of fresh seafood, as well as Chinese clay-pot specials and satay.

RIVER CAFE
Kuching Waterfront (next to Chinese History Museum)

Unfortunately, this attractive riverside café doesn't open until 3pm; for something to keep you going until supper time, try the excellent *popiah*, fresh spring rolls made to Aunty Yen's secret recipe. The cappuccino and ice creams are also recommended.

Chinese

MIN HONG KEE
157 Jalan Padungan

The best breakfasts in Kuching are found in this busy coffee shop, a 10-minute walk from the Holiday Inn. Excellent pork porridge, melting chee *chong fun* (stuffed rice-flour noodles), *tau suan* (split green pea porridge with deep-fried cruller or *yu tiaow*) and good roast poultry and pork.

LIFE CAFE
108 Ewe Hai Street
At the Leboh Temple end of Carpenter Street, this attractive small teahouse/ restaurant specialises in Chinese teas and coffee, and a few simple dishes such as vegetarian pot-sticker dumplings and fried rice. Iced passionfruit tea is excellent. Closed Tuesday.

JALAN CARPENTER CHINESE STALLS
Jalan Carpenter, opposite the Chinese temple
Look carefully at the back of this roofed-over cluster of stalls and you'll see the stage where Chinese opera used to be performed in front of the brilliantly decorated temple opposite. Excellent *kueh chap* (rice-flour noodle soup with pork and egg) until about 11am only at the stall on the front left. Also popular fish and prawn-ball soup, and many Chinese noodle dishes.

RIVERSIDE ENTERPRISE
32 Main Bazaar
Clean little café with friendly owners who'll lend you the newspaper to read while you eat. They rustle up anything from *laksa* to scrambled egg with toast and coconut jam (*kaya*); my favourite is Foochow Mee Sua: noodles with chicken and mushrooms.

MARIE CAFE
Jalan Ban Hock
About a 10-minute walk from the Waterfront, this is a popular place

for breakfast, particularly the *laksa*. Other specials available for lunch chalked up on a board. Closed at night.

TOH YUEN
Kuching Hilton, Jalan Tunku Abdul Rahman
Elegant Chinese restaurant with a delicious *dim sum* luncheon buffet and special food promotions from time to time. More pricey than most.

Western

THE WATERFRONT CAFE
Kuching Hilton, Jalan Tunku Abdur Rahman
My favourite place when I'm dying for a salad, served with excellent bread and rolls. Good-value lunch buffet with both local and Western food; sumptuous high tea.

Indian

GREEN VEGETARIAN RESTAURANT
16 Main Bazaar
No longer solely vegetarian, this southern Indian restaurant also offers meat, fish and poultry. For breakfast, try the *dosai* (rice and dhal-flour pancakes) with fresh coconut chutney; at lunch, the rice with spiced vegetable dishes and iced salty yogurt (*lassi*) girds your loins for the rest of the day. Clean, functional and very cheap.

BISMILLAH RESTAURANT
Lebuh Khoo Hun Yeang
Despite the Muslim name, this restaurant tucked away behind the central police station also offers northern Indian food, including tandoor baked breads (*naan*) and chicken. Muslim favourites include biryani and a range of curries.

NATIONAL ISLAMIC CAFE
Jalan Carpenter, near the post office
A real classic, offering inexpensive Malaysian Indian food, including

Canteen cooking

'Indian *rojak*' (deep-fried savouries with a rich, sweetish sauce). Flaky breads such as plain *roti canai* or *roti telor*, with an egg thrown in, make an excellent breakfast.

Sibu

Most visitors pause at Sibu only long enough to grab a quick meal before catching an express boat up the River Rajang. A pity, because Sibu has some very good food, and the night market is full of delicious take-away munchies. Tasty Malay food (curries, spiced vegetable dishes and rice) are good at the Gerai Makanan Muslim next to the Express Boat Wharf.

HOCK CHO LAU RESTAURANT
Jalan Blacksmith
Popular Chinese restaurant where the Hangchow duck, bean-curd soup and Foochow fried noodles (you're in the heart of Foochow territory here) are all recommended.

JIA BIN CAFE
Next to Sibu fire station
Highly regarded by the locals for its Kam Pua noodles.

Miri

Miri has always been an affluent town with a good range of Chinese and Western restaurants. What isn't well known is that some of the most interesting Malay food in Sarawak can be found here too. Some of the best places are located farther out of town on the road north, at new commercial centres. Those more easily accessible include the following four places:

A classic café

MAXIM'S
Pujut-Lutong Highway, next to Bintang Plaza
Popular at night for its selection of Chinese food, served at outdoor tables. Easy to order as sample dishes are on display, plus a variety of vegetables and fresh fish. Moderately priced.

CHATTERBOX COFFEE HOUSE
Mega Hotel, Jalan Maju
Surprisingly good Western food (thanks to the supervision of the French chef), as well as a range of Malaysian favourites at moderate prices. The steak with green peppercorn sauce is warmly recommended. Excellent walnut and dark bread, too.

TAMAN SEROJA FOOD STALLS
Jalan Brooke, near Brooke Inn
One or two stalls open at lunchtime, but this place comes into its own at night, with very tasty Malay food. Inexpensive and very good, but no beer.

JALAN OLEANDER FOOD STALLS
At the river end of Jalan Oleander (old China Street), near the temple and fish market.
It gets a tad warm at midday, but this cluster of stalls is excellent for home-style Malay dishes. Look for *pacheri nanas*, a tasty pineapple curry. Anything with squid is usually good, too.

Street-corner snacks

Nightlife

The nightlife in Sarawak is generally of the wholesome variety, particularly in comparison with racy Bangkok and glitzy Hong Kong. For most people, a good night out involves enjoying a slap-up meal, then going on to a session at one of the endlessly popular karaoke lounges, which you will find even in remote upriver towns such as Kapit. Laser-disc centres, where you can watch the latest movies, are also quite popular, although in the long-houses, people tend to watch satellite television.

There are, of course, some lively pubs, bars and discos, some featuring live music, especially in Kuching and Miri. Some of the more popular spots around Kuching include:

DAI ICHI KARAOKE
Jalan Tunku Abdur Rahman
Located above Pizza Hut, this up-market place is for karaoke fanatics – and there seem to be plenty of them in Kuching. Its fancy main lounge, plus 16 private rooms, have the latest sound equipment. There is a wide choice of songs.

DE TAVERN
Taman Sri Sarawak Mall (opposite Kuching Hilton)
This is a good spot to strike up conversation with local people, listen to music and enjoy a free sample of local rice wine (*tuak*).

MARGHERITA LOUNGE
Kuching Hilton
Sophisticated place for cocktails with good live music.

MARINA FUN PUB & DISCO
Jalan Ban Hock
You can enjoy live music until 2am, when the DJ takes over. Very popular at weekends.

PALM SUPPER LOUNGE & KARAOKE
Miramar Cinema Complex, Jalan Palm
Favourite spot with locals after a movie (which can be seen in the same complex), with public karaoke lounge plus private rooms.

PEPPERS DISCO
Kuching Hilton
Peppers is a perennial favourite. As well as the disco there's a karaoke lounge and pool table.

TRIBES
Holiday Inn Kuching
A bar and restaurant featuring ethnic food, decor and world music. Worth checking out.

TROPICAL PUB & BAR
Jln Abell (next to Benson's Seafood)
Decidedly local and great fun, if you can cope with the maximum volume, this is a popular haunt for those who love Malay/Indonesian music – locals and tourists alike.

The Tropical is a popular night spot

Calendar of Special Events

Sarawak celebrates the major national and religious festivals held elsewhere in multi-racial Malaysia, and adds a few of its own distinctive celebrations to boot. Many of the festivals follow a lunar calendar, so their date varies from year to year. For the latest information on festivals, contact the Visitors' Information Centre in Kuching, tel: (082) 410944.

Chinese New Year decorations

January to March

Chinese New Year: Celebrated in January or February, depending on the lunar calendar. For the month leading up to New Year, Sarawak's Chinese community spruce up their homes and offices, buy new clothes and send greeting cards.

The eve of New Year, the occasion for the family reunion dinner, is the start of the traditional 15-day period of celebrations. For the first two days, visits to family and friends and endless rounds of food are enjoyed. Af-ter this, lion dancers perform in front of homes and businesses to bring good fortune for the coming year (and, of course, to earn a few ringgit for the performers).

It's a colourful and noisy time of year, but don't even try to buy anything in a Chinese shop for the first two days of New Year. A special Chinese cultural show is held on the evening of Chap Goh Mei, the 15th day of the celebrations, in Kuching's Reservoir Park.

Thaipusam: Hindus in Kuching observe this spectacular festival in late January, when penitents bedeck themselves with spikes, spears and chariots before marching in procession from the river to a Hindu temple.

Hari Raya (Aidil Fitri): The major festival of the year for the Muslim community, this takes place at the end of the fasting month, Ramadan: the date varies from year to year, depending on the sighting of the new moon at the end of Ramadan. The festival begins with Muslims dressed in their finest traditional clothing offering prayers at mosques all over the state, followed by feasting and visits to family and friends.

Pesta Kaul: This is a Melanau festival, held in Mukah and Oya each March or April. It is a ritual cleansing of the villages and ensures the fishermen's safety over the coming year.

April to May

Balleh-Kapit Raft Safari: First held in early April in 1998, this colourful event is likely to become an annual celebration.

Vesak Day: The birth of Buddha is celebrated in May according to the Chinese lunar calendar, with special prayers and ritual washing of Buddha statues in the temples.

June to August

Gawai Dyak: Sarawak's official Gawai Dyak, celebrating the rice harvest, is observed by the state's Dyak communities (particularly the Iban) on 1 and 2 June, with 'open house'. Various longhouse communities hold their own celebrations depending upon the time of harvest (often in May), with copious amounts of food and rice wine (*tuak*) consumed. In Kuching, there are special cultural events and the crowning of a Gawai Queen.

Birthday of Yang di-Pertuan Agung: This festival, celebrated on 5 June, honours the supreme ruler of Malaysia.

Sarawak Regatta: Held in Kuching the weekend before National Day (31 August), this is an extremely popular event with local participants and spectators; there's a chance for tourists to join in a special paddling event.

The Rainforest World Music Festival: Scheduled for 28–30 August 1998, this will feature traditional and contemporary artistes from Borneo and around the region, as well as several performers of indigenous music from various parts of the world.

National Day: 31 August commemorates the founding of Malaysia with parades and traditional dances.

September to December

Rainforest Cup Mountain Bike Race: More for participants than spectators, this event celebrated its third birthday in 1998 in Kuching and looks likely to remain an annual fixture.

Deepavali: The beautiful Hindu Festival of Lights is celebrated in early November with the lighting of oil lamps (or strings of electric 'fairy lights') in the homes of Sarawak's Hindu Indians, who entertain their families and friends after prayers. A good time to buy rich Indian cakes and sweetmeats.

Christmas: The Malaysian tradition of 'open house', when friends of all races and religions are welcome to visit, is observed by Sarawak's Christians on Christmas Day. They normally attend religious services on Christmas Eve.

A local regatta

PRACTICAL Information

By Air

Kuching International Airport has direct flights from a number of destinations including Bandar Seri Begawan (Malaysia Airlines and Royal Brunei); Hong Kong (Dragonair); Manila (MAS); Perth (MAS); Seoul (MAS); Singapore (MAS and Singapore Airlines); and Tokyo (MAS). As Royal Brunei (which offers competitive fares) increases its international network, it is worth considering flying to Bandar Seri Begwan from other Asian destinations, Australia or Europe, and taking connecting flights to Sarawak. MAS offers a Discover Malaysia Pass (currently US$199), which enables visitors to fly to any five destinations within Malaysia.

From the airport the hotel district is about 20 minutes away. Vouchers are issued for taxi rides, but if you go to the taxi line it can be slightly cheaper. A half-hourly Sarawak Transport Company bus (No 12A) leaves from the airport.

By Road

There are two buses daily between Pontianak (West Kalimantan) and Kuching; the journey takes about 10 hours. Five buses a day ply between Kuala Belait in southern Brunei — with road connections to Bandar Seri Begawan — and Miri (2 hours). There are also two mini-bus services from Bandar Seri Begawan to Miri (4 hours). Or take the daily bus from Kota Kinabalu in Sabah to Lawas, in northern Sarawak, then go by express boat to Limbang, regular speedboat to Brunei and, finally, bus or mini-bus to Miri.

Ferry dock

By Sea

There is no scheduled passenger shipping service to Kuching but it is possible to take the ferry from Kota Kinabalu to Labuan, join a connecting ferry to Brunei, then travel by road to Miri.

TRAVEL ESSENTIALS

When to Visit

Sarawak's climate is tropical, with generally high humidity. The usually dry months of June (when the Gawai celebrations are held), July, August and September are perhaps the best time to visit. The rainy season, from November to March, usually brings brief but heavy showers, especially in the Kuching district and in Gunung Mulu National Park.

Visas and Passports

Passports must be valid for at least six months from your date of arrival. The state has its own immigration control, so even if you are coming from Peninsular Malaysia or neighbouring Sabah, you must go through immigration control. Visas are normally issued on arrival for 30 days, and can be extended for another 60 days at the Immigration Department in Kuching or Miri.

Citizens of Commonwealth countries, ASEAN, Ireland, Switzerland, the Netherlands and Liechtenstein do not need a visa to enter Sarawak. Nationals of the USA and many Western European countries are also exempt for a visit not exceeding three months. Visa requirements change from time to time: check with your nearest Malaysian embassy or consulate before travelling.

Customs and Duty-free

There is no duty-free allowance for visitors arriving from Peninsular Malaysia, Sabah or Singapore. Those arriving from other destinations, including neighbouring Brunei, may bring in 250g of tobacco or cigars, or 200 cigarettes, plus a one-quart bottle of alcohol. Pornography, weapons and walkie-talkies are prohibited; possession of narcotics and other illegal drugs carries the death sentence. Firearms are subject to licensing.

Vaccinations

Sarawak enjoys a high standard of health and vaccinations are not necessary. Visitors are required to produce a certificate of vaccination against yellow fever if they are travelling from an infected area.

Clothing and Equipment

Comfortable cotton clothing is ideal for Sarawak's tropical climate; wearing synthetics may make you feel you're encased in a plastic bag. Respect local standards of modesty: women should only wear very short skirts or brief shorts when in a resort. Cotton T-shirts or shirts, Bermuda shorts or skirts are ideal for everyday wear, and a sunhat (which can be bought locally) is strongly advised. If visiting a longhouse, a longer skirt, long pants or even a sarong are recommended for women.

An umbrella, for protection against both sun and rain, greatly adds to comfort, as does a pair of good sunglasses. Bring a light jacket to wear on express boats or long-distance buses, where the air-conditioning is often set to almost Arctic levels, and for early-morning travel by open longboat.

Trekkers will find that shorts and T-shirts are generally adequate; full 'jungle gear' of long-sleeved shirts and long pants is advisable only in leech-infested areas. A pair of comfortable, quick-drying trainers with a good grip is preferable to heavy leather boots, which are difficult to dry out in the humid climate. A lightweight sweater is advisable for evenings in higher altitudes, such as the Bario Highlands. If you're planning to go trekking, bring a lightweight sleeping bag and perhaps a compressed foam pad. You'll also need a good torch (flashlight) and batteries, water bottle, mosquito repellent and a basic medical kit.

Electricity

Power is 220V, 50 cycles; power plugs are of the three-pin variety, although adaptors are available in major hotels for appliances with two-pin plugs. Electricity is available in all towns and national parks; even the most remote longhouse has its own generator, operated for a few hours each evening.

Loading the four-wheel drive

Time

Sarawak time is 8 hours ahead of GMT and in the same time zone as the rest of Malaysia, Singapore and Hong Kong.

GETTING ACQUAINTED

Geography

Sarawak covers an area of 124,450 sq km (48,000 sq miles), making it by far the largest state in Malaysia. Lying just north of the equator, it is bordered on the south and east by Kalimantan, the Indonesian portion of Borneo, the world's third largest island. Sarawak wraps around Brunei's two separate portions and borders with the Malaysian state of Sabah in the north. Many of the coastal areas consist of peat swamp, with extensive river networks providing the most practical means of transport even today. Limestone outcrops and low hills are found in some areas of this coastal flood plain, while to the east, the land rises to hills, mountains and deep valleys. The massive limestone outcrops at Gunung Mulu are among the world's largest, although the highest mountain in the state, Gunung Murud, is a modest 2,423m (7,950ft). Sarawak has some of the most complex, luxuriant rainforests in the world.

Climate

Sarawak enjoys a tropical climate ranging in lowland areas from around 22°C to 32°C (73°F to 90°F), with relative humidity from 80 to 95 percent. The rainy season (usually referred to by its Iban name, *landas*) is between November and March, reaching a peak in December and January. Kuching experiences more rainfall than any other Malaysian city, although showers are generally brief.

Culture and Customs

The people of Sarawak are among the most welcoming in the world and will often break into a warm smile at the mere sight of a visitor. Thanks to the cultural diversity of the state, with 27 different ethnic and religious groups living in harmony, people are tolerant of any unwitting breaches of etiquette. However, it helps to observe a few simple points.

Always remove your shoes before entering a house, or leave them at the top of the stairs when arriving at a longhouse. It is considered rude to point with the finger; use your entire closed hand to indicate direction. Muslims consider the left hand unclean, so always use the right hand when giving or taking anything and when eating. Losing one's temper is considered the height of bad manners, and public displays of affection are an embarrassment. Nude sunbathing and skinny-dipping are totally unacceptable; always wrap yourself in a sarong if you intend bathing in a river outside a longhouse.

Visiting a Longhouse

Even if you are going with a tour operator, you should take gifts. Cigarettes and, unless it's a dry longhouse, inexpensive alcohol – Sahib 'whisky' and the lethal Chinese brand of arak, Cap Ah Pek – are appreciated by the men. For women, take illustrated magazines from your own country (or magazines in Malay), towels, sarongs, attractive soap, shampoo and talcum powder. Many people take sweets and snack food for children, but group games and colouring books are more lasting. Having postcards from your homeland, as well as family photos, provides a great conversation piece.

Be sure to pack mosquito repellent, hat, torch (flashlight), sunglasses, umbrella, towel and sarong. Wear Velcro-fastening sandals rather than trainers – your feet are sure to get wet and sandals dry out more quickly. Put all your personal belongings (including camera gear) inside plastic bags in a soft bag or backpack: it's almost impossible to remain dry when travelling upriver by longboat.

A guide, if you have one, will explain basic longhouse etiquette. Remember that

Tuak – the national drink

A city bank

you're visiting someone's home and don't go into private rooms or take photographs without asking. Never walk the length of a longhouse without stopping at least once to chat, as it's bad luck to go directly from one end to the other. Behave with consideration and courtesy and you'll be made to feel most welcome.

MONEY MATTERS

Currency

The Malaysian dollar or ringgit (abbreviated to RM) is divided into 100 cents (sen). Bank notes, in different colours, come in several denominations from RM2 to RM1,000. Coins are available in 1, 5, 10, 20 and 50 sen, as well as the bronze-coloured RM1. You can bring in and take out an unlimited amount of Malaysian currency. Exchange rates fluctuate, and during the latter half of 1997, the ringgit depreciated significantly against the US$. Check a newspaper, bank or money changer for the current rates, or if you are on the Internet, look for the currency converter in the travel section of CNN (http://www.cnn.com).

Credit Cards

Major credit cards such as American Express, Diners Club, Mastercard and Visa are accepted at large hotels and major restaurants in Kuching, Damai Beach and Sibu. Some remote resorts, such as the Royal Mulu, the Hilton Batang Ai and Pelagus Rapids, also accept credit cards. Cash is preferable elsewhere, and is essential for all national park reservations.

Money Changers

You can change major foreign currencies and travellers' cheques at most banks, but the best rate of exchange for both is at registered money changers, preferably in Kuching or Miri, where they are more easily located and offer better rates. Two of the most reliable money changers in Kuching, who will exchange currencies not acceptable in some hotels (such as the French franc), are Mohamad Yahia, on the lower ground floor of Sarawak Plaza, next to the Kuching Holiday Inn (open 10am–9pm); and Majid & Sons, 45 Jalan India (open 9am–7.30pm).

Tipping

There is a 10 percent service charge and a 5 percent government tax on all hotel bills, as well as in restaurants that are classified as 'tourist class'. Tipping is not an established local custom. However, bellboys and room-service staff in the more expensive hotels appreciate a tip of RM1–RM2.

GETTING AROUND

By Air

Places within Sarawak are well connected by a network of domestic MAS flights which serve Kuching, Sibu, Bintulu, Miri and Gunung Mulu (the latter also served by Merpati-Intan and Royal Brunei). The MAS Rural Air Services flies Twin Otters to a large number of destinations within Sarawak; those of greatest interest to visitors include flights from Miri (to Marudi, Gunung Mulu, Bario, Long Lellang, Long Seridan, Long Banga, Lawas and Limbang), from Limbang (to Bario), from Lawas (to Ba Kelalan) and from Sibu (Kapit and Mukah).

Taxis

Taxis do not use meters, so try to establish the fare in advance. They don't cruise the streets, so it's often difficult to locate one, especially in Kuching. Taxi ranks outside the Kuching Holiday Inn and Crowne Plaza Riverside Kuching, and at the other end of Main Bazaar (Jalan Gambier/Leboh Jawa) are the best bets. Or call (082) 343343, (082) 342255, (082) 348898,

(082) 367898, (016) 888 2255 or (010) 886 6224. Often it saves time and frustration to have the taxi stay with you; you can negotiate an hourly or half-day rate. The minimum fare in Kuching (1998 rates) is RM5; the fare to the airport is RM15. In smaller towns, taxi ranks are normally next to the long-distance bus stations.

Buses

The bus system in Kuching can be somewhat confusing as there is no central terminus and different companies leave from different parts of town. Where travel by bus is recommended, the departure point is given in the individual itineraries. Air-conditioned express buses join Kuching with towns to the east and north, although it is quicker and more comfortable to take the express boat or plane from Kuching to Sibu. Express buses linking Sibu with Bintulu, bypassing Niah en route for Miri, are an inexpensive and relatively comfortable alternative to flying. Buses are often very cold, though, so bring a jacket. Check the *Sarawak Tribune* for latest timetables. Non-air-conditioned country buses leave every 2–4 hours from Kuching.

Express boat service

Express Boats

You haven't really visited Sarawak if you haven't taken an express boat. They ply the coast and rivers between Kuching and Sibu, and roar up the Rajang and Baram rivers. The air-conditioning is generally set to freezing and videos are played back to back during the journey, making you long for earplugs. But this is the way the locals travel; it's quicker than the bus to Sibu and is often the only way to reach

some coastal or upriver villages. Travelling in an open longboat, with an outboard engine, is more pleasurable and allows you to see more of your surroundings. Departures from Kuching are subject to the tides; check the *Sarawak Tribune* for the current timetables, or call Express Bahagia, (tel: 082-421948) or Concord Marine, (tel: 082-412561/412551). To get to the express boat jetty at Pending, take a taxi or bus No 19 from the Kuching Waterfront.

Car Rental

Hiring a car for exploring the Kuching area and the nearby districts is an excellent idea, although not recommended for long distances. Drive on the left-hand side of the road; major roads are well signposted. Prices range between RM140 and RM350 a day. Advance reservation is highly recommended.

Mayflower Car Rental
Lot 4.24A, 4th floor, Bangunan Satok, Jalan Satok
Tel: (082) 410110/410117;
Fax: (082) 575233
Mayflower is also located at Kuching International Airport.

Pronto Car Rental
1st floor, 98 Jalan Padungan
Tel: (082) 236889/237889; after hours 010-8879468; Fax: (082) 236889
Pronto is also located at Kuching International Airport.

HOURS AND HOLIDAYS

Business Hours

Local markets and provision stores generally open early in the morning; supermarkets and department stores open seven days a week, 9am–9pm. Other private-sector business and offices normally operate 9am–5pm.

Government offices open Monday to Thursday, 8am–12.45pm, 2pm–4.30pm; Friday, 8am–11.30am, 2pm–4.30pm; Saturday, 8am–12.45pm.

Bank opening hours are Monday to Friday, 9.30am–3.30pm; Saturday, 9.30am–11.30am.

Celebrating Chinese New Year

Public Holidays

The following dates are official public holidays in Sarawak. There are many other festivals whose dates are determined by the lunar calendar; check with the Visitors' Information Centre (tel: 082-416700) for details.

New Year's Day	1 January
Chinese New Year	January/February
Good Friday	April; date variable
Labour Day	1 May
Gawai Dyak	1 & 2 June
The King's Birthday	5 June
National Day	31 August
Deepavali	early November
Christmas Day	25 December

ACCOMMODATION

There is a good range of accommodation in Sarawak, from luxurious resorts and sophisticated city hotels to budget-priced establishments. Accommodation at national parks – with the exception of Gunung Mulu National Park, where a wide range of accommodation is located just outside the border – is run by the National Parks and Wildlife Department. Book your accommodation through the nearest Visitors' Information Centre (*see page 86*).

Unless otherwise noted, all the hotels mentioned in the listings here have en-suite bathrooms, air-conditioning and television. Published daily rates for a standard double room are categorised as follows: *$$$$* = US$100 and above; *$$$* = US$50–US$99; *$$* = US$25–49; *$* = less than US$25.

The Kuching Hilton

Kuching

KUCHING HILTON INTERNATIONAL
Jalan Tunku Abdul Ruhman
Tel: (082) 248200; Fax: (082) 428984
Considered Kuching's premier hotel; convenient riverside location and all the facilities expected of a five-star hotel. Lunchtime buffet in the Waterfront Café is good value. *$$$$*

HOLIDAY INN KUCHING
Jalan Tunku Abdul Rahman
Tel: (082) 423111; Fax: (082) 426169
Right on the river, Kuching's very first international-standard hotel is still a comfortable place to stay. A shuttle bus service connects with the two Holiday Inn resorts, Damai Beach and Damai Lagoon. *$$$$*

CROWNE PLAZA RIVERSIDE KUCHING
Jalan Tunku Abdul Rahman
Tel: (082) 247777; Fax: (082) 425858
Luxurious hotel in a complex containing a modern shopping precinct, bowling centre and cineplex. Twinned with the two Holiday Inn Damai resorts, which can be reached by shuttle bus. *$$$$*

Holiday Inn's Damai Beach resort

HOTEL GRAND CONTINENTAL
Lot 42, Section 46 Jalan Ban Hock
Tel: (082) 230399; Fax: (082) 230339
A RM5 taxi ride from the Waterfront area
of Kuching, this new hotel (with swimming
pool) is favoured by local businessmen.
Good value; ask for a discount. *$$$*

BORNEO HOTEL
30 Jalan Tabuan
Tel: (082) 244122; Fax: (082) 254848
The best of Kuching's moderately priced
hotels, within easy walking distance of
everything. Good food and friendly service,
although rooms are rather small. *$$*

TELANG USAN HOTEL
Off Jalan Ban Hock
Tel: (082) 415588; Fax: (082) 425316
A little further out of town than Borneo
Hotel; very friendly, comfortable and mod-
erately priced. *$$*

GREEN MOUNTAIN LODGING HOUSE
1 Jalan Green Hill
Tel: (082) 416320; Fax: (082) 246342
Popular with backpackers and conveniently
located, rooms have air-conditioning and
hot water. *$*

ANGLICAN GUEST HOUSE
St Thomas Cathedral
Jalan Tun Haji Openg
Tel: (082) 414027
Beautifully located guesthouse; five rooms
with shared fridge, showers and toilets.
No air-conditioning. Call in advance. *$*

B&B INN
1st & 2nd floor, Jalan Tabuan
Tel: (082) 237366
Hostel for budget travellers; US$5 for a
bed in a 6-bed dormitory, or around US$8
for a room, inclusive of breakfast. *$*

Damai

HOLIDAY INN DAMAI LAGOON RESORT
Tel: (082) 846900
Fax: (082) 846901
Rooms and suites in multi-storey blocks,
chalets located near huge lagoon-style pool
and beach; offers a wide range of water-
sports and other activities. Within easy
walking distance of the Sarawak Cultural
Village. *$$$*

HOLIDAY INN DAMAI BEACH RESORT
Tel: (082) 846999
Fax: (082) 846777
Perhaps the nicest spot to stay in Damai.
The newer hilltop rooms and suites have
stunning views and their own pool; the
main facilities and other accommodation
are located near the beach. *$$$*

SANTUBONG KUCHING RESORT
Tel: (082) 846888
Fax (082) 846666
Less luxurious than the other two Damai
Beach resorts, but offers a range of water-
sports and other activities. *$$$*

Sibu

TANAHMAS HOTEL
Jalan Kampung Nyabor
Tel: (084) 333188; Fax: (084) 333288
Sibu's top hotel, much favoured by local
businessmen. *$$$*

HOTEL CAPITOL 88
19 Jalan Wong Nai Siong
Tel: (084) 336444; Fax: (084) 311706
Near the post office about 10 minutes'
walk from the express boat jetty; good
value for comfortable, clean, air-conditioned
rooms. *$*

HOTEL RIA
21 Jalan Channel
Tel: (084) 326622
Budget hotel with the advantage of being
closest to the express boat jetty. *$*

Miri

HOLIDAY INN MIRI
Jalan Temenggong Datuk Oyong
Tel: (085) 418888; Fax: (085) 419999
Five-star comfort right on the beach at the mouth of the Miri river. Popular with businessmen. *$$$*

RIHGA ROYAL HOTEL
Jalan Temenggong Datuk Oyong
Tel: (085) 421121; Fax: (085) 421099
This popular, beachfront resort has the largest swimming pool in the country. Rooms in the low-rise wings are recommended. *$$$*

DYNASTY HOTEL
Jalan Pujut-Lutong
Tel: (085) 421111; Fax: (085) 422222
The best hotel in Miri after the two five-star properties on the beach; next to a shopping complex and within walking distance of everything. *$$$*

MEGA HOTEL
Jalan Maju
Tel: (085) 432432; Fax: (085) 433433
One of the newer four-star hotels; offers comfortable rooms, a convenient location, moderate prices and some of the best Western food in town. A popular tour operator, Tropical Adventure, is located on the premises. *$$*

BROOKE INN
14 Jalan Brooke
Tel: (085) 412881; Fax: (085) 420899
My favourite budget hotel in Sarawak; friendly staff; within walking distance of the town bus station and Visitors' Information Centre; next door to good Malay food stalls (Taman Seroja). *$*

Bario

TARAWES
Opposite Bario shops, about 15 minutes' walk from the airport.
A simple but comfortable guesthouse run by a friendly family; son John and his English wife Karen are very helpful. *$*

Ba Kelalan

APPLE LODGE
Tel: (085) 436566; Fax: (085) 414146

Facing the landing strip in Buduk Nur, this new, very clean and comfortable wooden lodge has shared bathing and toilet facilities, a lounge and restaurant. *$*

Royal Mulu Lodge

Gunung Mulu

ROYAL MULU LODGE
Tel: (085) 421121; Fax: (085) 425057
Almost indecent comfort in the midst of the rainforest; a beautiful resort located on the edge of Gunung Mulu National Park; warmly recommended. *$$$*

Mukah

KING ING HOTEL
Tel: (084) 871400
Good location by the River Mukah, near the town's old bazaar and opposite the Chinese temple. The King Ing is the best hotel in town. *$*

Bintulu

PLAZA HOTEL
Tel: (086) 335111; Fax: (086) 332742
Four-star hotel frequented by businessmen and the few tourists passing through Bintulu. A good place for Western food. *$$$*

HOOVER INN
Jalan Abang Galau
Tel: (086) 337166
The best of the moderately priced establishments and conveniently located. *$$*

SUNLIGHT INN
Situated between Jalan Abang Galau and Jalan Sommerville
Tel: (086) 332677
Just five minutes' walk from the airport, the Sunlight Inn is one of the better budget hotels in town. *$*

Batang Ai

HILTON BATANG AI RESORT

Tel: (083) 584388; Fax: (083) 584399
One of the most attractively designed resorts in Sarawak, the Hilton Batang Ai Resort is set in the middle of the 'lake' formed by the Batang Ai hydro dam. It offers luxurious comfort, a swimming pool and a range of activities, which include guided jungle treks. It also makes an ideal jumping-off point for day trips or overnight stays in nearby Iban longhouses. *$$$*

Rajang River

PELAGUS RAPIDS RESORT

Tel: (082) 238033; Fax: (082) 238050
Reached via Kapit, Pelagus is an attractive longhouse-style resort set in virgin forest. Escorted jungle treks and trips to a nearby Iban longhouse and waterfall can be arranged. Comfortable facilities and perfect peace can be guaranteed at this pleasant resort. *$$*

Always wear a hat in the sun

HEALTH AND HYGIENE

General Health

Sarawak has a high standard of hygiene and visitors can safely eat and drink almost anywhere. Tap water is safe in Kuching and the towns; in remote areas, local people always boil drinking water. Locally bottled water is widely available. Drink plenty of it to avoid dehydration.

Malaria is rarely encountered in Sarawak, but a repellent is recommended against the irritation of mosquitoes. Bring your own, although they can usually be found in Kuching pharmacies. Take care to avoid sunburn, even on overcast days. Always use sunscreen in coastal areas and in the Bario Highlands. Carry antiseptic or antibiotic ointment and a diarrhoea remedy (the herbal Chinese Po Chai or Po Chee pills available in any Chinese store are usually effective).

Pharmacies

Patent medicines are widely available and pharmacies in major towns always have a trained pharmacist on duty. Many medicines are also available in general stores even in remote areas.

Clinics and Hospitals

Sarawak has an excellent system of health care, with clinics even in remote upriver regions dispensing advice and medication. Doctors and most nursing staff speak English, and public hospitals and clinics accept foreign patients. You can visit an outpatient centre at a hospital or ask your hotel to recommend a local doctor. One conveniently located and well-regarded private clinic, the Doctor's Clinic, is at the temple end of Kuching's Main Bazaar, opposite the Chinese History Museum.

There are two excellent private hospitals offering outpatient services in Kuching. Normah Medical Centre (tel: 082 440055), on Jalan Datuk Patinggi, is on the north side of the River Sarawak (about RM12–15 by taxi). Timberland Medical Centre (tel: 082 234991), is on Jalan Rock in the southern part of Kuching (about RM7 by taxi).

COMMUNICATIONS AND NEWS

Post and Telecommunications

The main post office in Kuching is currently crammed into a lovely old colonial building, which is charming but hopelessly crowded. Register mail if it is important; it costs only another RM1.

Malaysia has an efficient telecommunications system with coin or card-operated phones in towns, villages and sometimes alongside main roads near longhouses. Although you can make international calls from your hotel, it's cheaper to use public IDD telephones. Public phones are operated by two different companies and require

A rural postbox

and suffix *an*, we get the noun *kedudukan*, which means 'position'. By adding a different prefix, *pen*, we get another noun, *penduduk*, which means 'inhabitant'. Adding an *i* after *duduk* turns it into an active verb ('to sit'), while *menduduki* is a present continuous verb.

For the most part, words are pronounced as they are spelt. In general, the pronunciation is the same as in English, with a few exceptions.

In Bahasa Malaysia, 'a' is pronounced 'ar' as in 'tar'. The letter 'e' has an 'er' sound, as in 'reserve'. You will also find that 'c' is pronounced 'ch' as in 'chair'; the letter 'g' is always hard, as in 'gun' and 'garden', not as in 'ginger'; and 'sy' is pronounced 'sh'.

The language uses two distinct scripts: Jawi and Rumi. Jawi is the Arabic form of writing; Rumi the Roman alphabet, considered the easier of the two and also the official script of the country.

Here is a small vocabulary to get you on your way.

two different phone cards, sold in shops displaying a Telekom or Uniphone card sign.

Useful numbers (Kuching)

Police/Tourist Police:	(082) 241222
Long-distance Enquiries:	101
Directory Service:	103
Access for IDD calls:	00
Immigration:	(082) 245661

Media

The major English-language daily available in Sarawak is the *Sarawak Tribune*, which is particularly useful for express boat and express bus timetables. The *Borneo Post* has local and international news, while several of the peninsular Malaysian newspapers (*New Straits Times, The Star, The Sun*) are also available. Sarawak receives satellite transmission of Peninsular Malaysian TV (TV 3 carries the largest number of English-language programmes) and many hotels and restaurants in remote towns subscribe to Astro or Mega TV, offering a range of channels (including CNN) 24 hours a day.

LANGUAGE

The Malay language, or Bahasa Malaysia, is polysyllabic, with variations in syllables to convey changes in meaning, unlike tonal languages such as Mandarin, Cantonese and Thai. For example, *duduk* (meaning 'sit') is a verb. By adding the prefix *ke*

Numbers

1	*Satu*
2	*Dua*
3	*Tiga*
4	*Empat*
5	*Lima*
6	*Enam*
7	*Tujuh*
8	*Lapan*
9	*Sembilan*
10	*Sepuluh*
11	*Sebelas*
12	*Dua belas*
13	*Tiga belas*
20	*Dua puluh*
21	*Dua puluh satu*
100	*Seratus*
200	*Dua ratus*
1,000	*Seribu*

Greetings and other phrases

How do you do?	*Apa khabar?*
Good morning	*Selamat pagi*
Good afternoon	*Selamat petang*
Good evening	*Selamat malam*
Goodbye	*Selamat tinggal*
Bon voyage	*Selamat jalan*
Fine/good	*Baik*

Thank you	Terima kasih
Please	Tolong/sila
Excuse me	Maafkan saya
I am sorry	Saya minta maaf
Yes	Ya
No	Tidak

Pronouns
I	Saya
You	Anda/awak
He/she	Dia
We	Kami
They	Mereka

Forms of address
Mr	Encik
Mrs	Puan
Miss	Cik

Directions and travel
Where	Di mana
Right	Kanan
Left	Kiri
Turn	Belok
Go	Pergi
Stop	Berhenti
Follow	Ikut
Near	Dekat
Far	Jauh
Inside	Dalam
Outside	Luar
Front	Hadapan
Behind	Belakang
Here	Sini
There	Sana
Road/street	Jalan
Bridge	Jambatan

Junction	Simpang
North	Utara
South	Selatan
East	Timur
West	Barat

Useful phrases
How much?	Berapa harganya?
Can you help me?	Bolehkah encik tolong saya?
Where is this place?	Di mana tempat ini?
How far?	Berapa jauh?
I want to go to...	Saya hendak pergi ke...
Stop here	Tolong berhenti sini
Expensive	Mahal
Lower the price	Kurang harganya
Too big	Besar sangat
Too small	Kecil sangat
Any other colour?	Ada warna lain?

Other handy words
Drink	Minum (verb)
	Minuman (noun: food)
Eat	Makan (verb),
	Makanan (noun)
Fruit	Buah-buahan
Water	Air
Have	Ada
Don't have	Tidak ada
Toilet	Tandas
Hot (spicy)	Pedas
Hot (heat)	Panas
Cold	Sejuk
Sweet	Manis
Sour	Masam
Delicious	Sedap
Clean	Bersih
Dirty	Kotor
Open	Buka
Close	Tutup
Never	Tidak pernah
Often	Selalu
Sometimes	Kadang-kadang

Sarawak has an excellent network of 10 national parks and two wildlife centres. There are also several nature reserves which are smaller in scale and do not have accommodation. Accommodation is available at Bako; Gunung Gading; Gunung

Keeping in touch

Jet skiing is popular

Mulu; Kubah; Lambir Hills; Matang; Niah and Similajau. Kitchen facilities are available in most chalets and hostels, most of which have fridges; you may need to request the loan of kitchen utensils. Bookings are made at the nearest Visitors' Information Centre (*see page 86*).

Photography

Because of the heat and humidity, carry your camera equipment in a closed bag with plenty of silica gel, and cover it with a plastic bag when travelling in a longboat or trekking.

Print film is widely available; for slide film, it's best to stock up in Kuching. Fuji Image Plaza on the first floor of Sarawak Plaza, Kuching, has a range of high-speed Fujichrome film. For camera repair and a good range of equipment, try Empress Studio, 1B Jalan India, Kuching.

SPORTS

The most popular resort sports include windsurfing, water-skiing, jet skiing, tennis, squash, swimming and cycling. The resorts at Damai Beach as well as at Miri and, to a lesser extent, Batang Ai, offer the best range of options.

Fishing trips can be arranged off Santubong, near Damai Beach, but don't expect spectacular results. The best place for deep-sea fishing is to the far southwest of Sarawak, near Tanjung Datu; be aware, however, that the nearby Talang islands are a marine reserve and should not be fished.

Gunung Mulu National Park offers excellent opportunities for adventure caving (*see* Itinerary 12, *page 54*, for details) as well as for trekking, kayaking and climbing. The most enjoyable trekking is probably in the Kelabit Highlands, in northeastern Sarawak near the Indonesian border, where the refreshing climate of the lower montane rainforest contrasts pleasantly with the humidity of the lowland forest.

Scuba diving, a relatively new sport in Sarawak, is now possible thanks to the availability of a live-aboard boat visiting the Luconia Shoals in the South China Sea far to the northwest of Sarawak. (Other regions off Sarawak's coast do not offer good diving.) At the moment, Tropical Adventure (*see page 86*) is the only company offering dive trips to Luconia, from April to October.

Another new but increasingly popular sport is mountain biking, and although the professionals challenge themselves in places like Batang Ai and Gunung Mulu, most locals (and visitors) find that a number of trails around Kuching are worth pursuing. Bikes can be rented from Borneo Adventure in Kuching (*see page 86*), who will also help plan itineraries or longer biking tours.

There are three golf courses in the Kuching area, plus a 9-hole course in Miri. The best of these is the Arnold Palmer-designed Damai Golf Course in Santubong, conveniently close to the resorts. Closer to Kuching is the 18-hole Kelab Golf Sarawak; ask your hotel receptionist to arrange a game.

If meeting the locals and discovering the environs of Kuching while ploughing through mud and scrub or farmland appeals, you could try the Hash House Harriers. The Kuching chapter has regular runs on Tuesday, Wednesday and Saturday, followed by the popular 'On On', a meal and a drink or two (or three). Contact Jennifer Yap, tel: (082) 411694 or Tom Leng tel: (082) 363096.

TOURIST INFORMATION

Information Centres

There are Visitors' Information Centres in the three major towns: Monday to Thursday, 8am–4.15pm; Friday, 8am–4.45pm; Saturday, 8am–12.45pm.

KUCHING
31 Jalan Masjid (just down from the new wing of the Sarawak Museum)
Tel: (082) 410944; Fax (082) 256301
E-mail: stb@po.jaring.my
(Bookings taken for Bako, Gunung Gading and Kubah National Parks)

A Visitors' Information Centre

SIBU
32 Cross Road (Ground Floor)
Tel: (084) 340980; Fax (084) 341280
E-mail: stbsibu@tm.net.my

MIRI
Lot 452, Jalan Melayu (by Miri bus station, opposite Taman Muhibbah)
Tel: (085) 434181 Fax: (085) 434179
E-mail: stb@po.jaring.my
(Bookings taken for Niah and Mulu.)

AIRLINE OFFICES

Kuching

DRAGONAIR
1st Floor, Wisma Bukit Mata Kuching, Jalan Tunku Abdur Rahman
Tel: (082) 233322

MALAYSIA AIRLINES
Jalan Song Thian Cheok
Tel: (082) 246622/244144

ROYAL BRUNEI
1st Floor, Rugayah Building Jalan Song Thian Cheok
Tel: (082) 243344/246288

SINGAPORE AIRLINES
Wisma Bukit Mata Kuching, Jalan Tunku Abdul Rahman
Tel: (082) 240266

Sibu

MALAYSIA AIRLINES
61 Jalan Tuanku Osman
Tel: (084) 326166

Miri

MALAYSIA AIRLINES
Lot 239, Beautiful Jade Centre
Tel: (085) 414144

TOUR OPERATORS AND GUIDES

Kuching

BORNEO ADVENTURE
55 Main Bazaar
Tel: (082) 245175/410569/415554;
Fax: (082) 422626
E-mail: bakch@po.jaring.my
This company has won several international awards for its sensitive approach to environmentally friendly tourism. It offers longhouse trips and tours to all regions of Sarawak.

IBANIKA EXPEDITION
Lot 435, Ground floor, Section 62, Lorong 9, Jalan Ang Cheng Ho
Tel: (082) 424022;
Fax: (082) 424021
E-mail: ibanika@ace.cdc.abu.com
This is a long-established company offering longhouse and general tours.

SAGA TRAVEL
D 47, Level 1, Taman Sri Sarawak Mall, Jalan Tunku Abdur Rahman
Tel: (082) 418705, 423429;
Fax: (082) 426299
E-mail: sagakch@po.jaring.my
Reliable operator offering a range of tours and good guides; especially recommended for trips west of Kuching.

TROPICAL ADVENTURE
1st floor, 17 Main Bazaar
Tel: (082) 413088; Fax: (082) 413104
See Miri listings (*page 87*) for further information.

Sibu

SAZHONG TRADING AND TRAVEL
4 Jalan Central
Tel: (084) 336017, 334222;
Fax: (084) 338031
Valuable help for trips to the Mukah region of the Sibu district.

Kapit

KAPIT ADVENTURE TOURS
11 Jalan Tan Sit Leong
Tel: (084) 796362; Fax: (084) 796655
Specialises in longhouse trips and offers a trek into Kalimantan.

Miri

BORNEO ADVENTURE
Unit 9, 15 Wisma Pelita,
Jalan Puchong
Tel: (085) 414935; Fax: (085) 419543
E-mail: bamyy@po.jaring.my
See Kuching listings for information.

BORNEO OVERLAND SERVICES
Lot 1089, 1st floor, Dayak Association Building, Jalan Merpati
Tel: (085) 421510; Fax (085) 416424
Small, friendly company specialising in northeastern Sarawak.

TROPICAL ADVENTURE
Ground floor, Mega Hotel,
Lot 907, Jalan Merbau
Tel: (085) 419337; Fax (085) 414503
E-mail: hthee@pc.jaring.my
Website: http://www.tropicaladv.com
One of the best operators for tours to Gunung Mulu National Park, especially adventure caving and the Headhunters' Trail. Also recommended for Bario Highlands trekking.

Bario

Experienced guides who will accompany you on treks in the Kelabit Highlands include the following: **James Pearson Mato Inan**, Pa Lungan, Bario 98050, Sarawak; and **Larry Bujang**, PO Box 33, Bario 98050, Sarawak. Both speak excellent English and are thoroughly experienced.

Ba Kelalan

Treks around the beautiful valley of Ba Kelalan can be arranged through: **Peng Ating**, Long Muda, Buduk Nur, Ba Kelalan, Lawas, Sarawak. Peng runs the small store/canteen to the right as you approach the airport terminal; he speaks perfect English.

Lawas to Ba Kelalan

SOUTHERN COMFORT
20km (12 miles) from Lawas town
Tel/Fax: (085) 493523
E-mail: ctx@tm.net.my
A small eco-tourism lodge offering an imaginative range of tours, including 4WD excursions in the highland rainforest region inhabited by the Lun Bawang tribe.

CONSULATES

AUSTRALIAN HONORARY CONSUL
Dr Philip Ting Ding Ing, Kuching
Tel: (082) 245661

BRITISH CONSULATE & TRADE OFFICE
Rugayah Building, Jalan Song Thian Cheok, Kuching
Tel: (082) 231320

CANADIAN CONSULATE
Level 12B, Wisma Ting Peck Khing,
1 Jalan Padungan, Kuching
Tel: (082) 23700, 233000

FURTHER READING

See pages 63–64 for where to buy books or to order them in advance.

Travel

Into the Heart of Borneo by O'Hanlon, Redmond, Edinburgh: The Salamander Press, 1984. Undoubtedly the funniest travel book ever written about Borneo.

A jungle guide prepares lunch

A Short Stroll Through Borneo by Barclay, James, London: Hodder & Stoughton, 1980. A simply written, perceptive and very readable account of travels in Sarawak and Kalimantan in Central Borneo.

The Best of Borneo Travel by King, Victor T (ed), Singapore: OUP, 1992. An anthology of some of the best travel writing on Borneo since the 16th century.

History and Culture

Borneo: The People of the Weeping Forest by Ave, Jan B and King, Victor T, Leiden: National Museum of Ethnology, 1986. A comprehensive look at the geography, administration, history and people of Borneo that adds greatly to an understanding of Sarawak.

A Kayan man

World Within by Harrisson, Tom, Singapore: OUP, 1986 (reprint). Now a classic, this is an account of the Kelabits of the Bario region during the Japanese Occupation in World War II.

Sarawak Crafts, Methods and Motifs by Munan, Heidi, Kuala Lumpur: OUP, 1989. A small, information-packed guide to Sarawak's handicrafts by a writer who has lived here for 30 years.

Sarawak Style by Ong, Edric and Tettoni, Luca, Singapore: Times Editions, 1996. Beautifully photographed with an in-

formative text on the cultural heritage of Sarawak's people.

Sarawak Cultural Legacy: A Living Tradition by Chin, Lucas and Mashman, Valerie (eds), Kuching: Society Atelier Sarawak, 1991. Excellent reference book on Sarawak's cultural traditions.

Culture Shock! Borneo by Munan, Heidi, Singapore: Times Books International, 1988. Part of a series intended for expatriates and visitors; advice on how to behave and insight on local customs.

Natural Man: A Record from Borneo by Hose, Charles, Singapore: OUP, 1988. A reprint of a 1912 work, this is a sympathetic and unbiased account by an English colonial administrator who served Rajah Charles Brooke for 23 years.

Penans: The Vanishing Nomads of Borneo by Lau, Dennis, Sabah: Interstate Publishing, 1987. Black and white photographs documenting a fast-vanishing way of life.

Nature

Wild Malaysia by Cubitt, Gerald and Payne, Junaidi, London: New Holland, 1990. Beautifully written by an expert who has spent more than a decade working for the World Wide Fund for Nature in Sarawak and Sabah; illustrated with magnificent photographs.

Orang-utan: Malaysia's Mascot by Payne, Junaidi and Andau, Mahedi, Kuala Lumpur: Berita Publishing, 1989. Delightful little book full of interesting information and photographs of these lovable apes.

Proboscis Monkeys of Borneo by Bennett, Elizabeth and Gombek, Francis, Kota Kinabalu: Natural History Publications, 1993. Comprehensive information, together with maps and some spectacular photographs.

Insight Guide to Southeast Asia Wildlife. Singapore: Apa Publications, 1991. Packed with information and stunning photographs, this has detailed information on Sarawak's national parks and nature reserves.

Pocket Guide to the Birds of Borneo by Francis, Charles M, Kuala Lumpur: The Sabah Society, 1984. An ideal companion for the bird lover in Sabah.

A dramatic rainforest waterfall

Index

ACKNOWLEDGMENTS

Photography Wendy Hutton *and*
         12 Sarawak Museum

Cover Design Derrick Lim
Cartography Berndtson & Berndtson

Insight Guides

Alaska
Alsace
Amazon Wildlife
American Southwest
Amsterdam
Argentina
Atlanta
Athens
Australia
Austria
Bahamas
Bali
Baltic States
Bangkok
Barbados
Barcelona
Bay of Naples
Beijing
Belgium
Belize
Berlin
Bermuda
Boston
Brazil
Brittany
Brussels
Budapest
Buenos Aires
Burgundy
Burma (Myanmar)
Cairo
Calcutta
California
Canada
Caribbean
Catalonia
Channel Islands
Chicago
Chile
China
Cologne
Continental Europe
Corsica
Costa Rica
Crete
Crossing America
Cuba
Cyprus
Czech & Slovak
  Republics
Delhi, Jaipur, Agra
Denmark

Dresden
Dublin
Düsseldorf
East African Wildlife
East Asia
Eastern Europe
Ecuador
Edinburgh
Egypt
Finland
Florence
Florida
France
Frankfurt
French Riviera
Gambia & Senegal
Germany
Glasgow
Gran Canaria
Great Barrier Reef
Great Britain
Greece
Greek Islands
Hamburg
Hawaii
Hong Kong
Hungary
Iceland
India
India's Western
  Himalaya
Indian Wildlife
Indonesia
Ireland
Israel
Istanbul
Italy
Jamaica
Japan
Java
Jerusalem
Jordan
Kathmandu
Kenya
Korea
Lisbon
Loire Valley
London
Los Angeles
Madeira
Madrid
Malaysia
Mallorca & Ibiza
Malta

Marine Life in the
  South China Sea
Melbourne
Mexico
Mexico City
Miami
Montreal
Morocco
Moscow
Munich
Namibia
Native America
Nepal
Netherlands
New England
New Orleans
New York City
New York State
New Zealand
Nile
Normandy
Northern California
Northern Spain
Norway
Oman & the UAE
Oxford
Old South
Pacific Northwest
Pakistan
Paris
Peru
Philadelphia
Philippines
Poland
Portugal
Prague
Provence
Puerto Rico
Rajasthan
Rhine
Rio de Janeiro
Rockies
Rome
Russia
St Petersburg
San Francisco
Sardinia
Scotland
Seattle
Sicily
Singapore
South Africa
South America
South Asia

South India
South Tyrol
Southeast Asia
Southeast Asia Wildlife
Southern California
Southern Spain
Spain
Sri Lanka
Sweden
Switzerland
Sydney
Taiwan
Tenerife
Texas
Thailand
Tokyo
Trinidad & Tobago
Tunisia
Turkey
Turkish Coast
Tuscany
Umbria
US National Parks East
US National Parks West
Vancouver
Venezuela
Venice
Vienna
Vietnam
Wales
Washington DC
Waterways of Europe
Wild West
Yemen

Insight Pocket Guides

Aegean Islands★
Algarve★
Alsace
Amsterdam★
Athens★
Atlanta★
Bahamas★
Baja Peninsula★
Bali★
Bali *Bird Walks*
Bangkok★
Barbados★
Barcelona★
Bavaria★
Beijing★
Berlin★
Bermuda★

Insight Guides

over every major destination in every continent.

Bhutan★
Boston★
British Columbia★
Brittany★
Brussels★
Budapest &
  Surroundings★
Canton★
Chiang Mai★
Chicago★
Corsica★
Costa Blanca★
Costa Brava★
Costa del
Sol/Marbella★
Costa Rica★
Crete★
Denmark★
Fiji★
Florence★
Florida★
Florida Keys★
French Riviera★
Gran Canaria★
Hawaii★
Hong Kong★
Hungary
Ibiza★
Ireland★
Ireland's Southwest★
Israel★
Istanbul★
Jakarta★
Jamaica★
Kathmandu *Bikes &*
  Hikes★
Kenya★
Kuala Lumpur★
Lisbon★
Loire Valley★
London★
Macau
Madrid★
Malacca
Maldives
Mallorca★
Malta★
Mexico City★
Miami★
Milan★
Montreal★
Morocco★
Moscow
Munich★

Nepal★
New Delhi
New Orleans★
New York City★
New Zealand★
Northern California★
Oslo/Bergen★
Paris★
Penang★
Phuket★
Prague★
Provence★
Puerto Rico★
Quebec★
Rhodes★
Rome★
Sabah★
St Petersburg★
San Francisco★
Sardinia
Scotland★
Seville★
Seychelles★
Sicily★
Sikkim
Singapore★
Southeast England
Southern California★
Southern Spain★
Sri Lanka★
Sydney★
Tenerife★
Thailand★
Tibet★
Toronto★
Tunisia★
Turkish Coast★
Tuscany★
Venice★
Vienna★
Vietnam★
Yogyakarta
Yucatan Peninsula★

★ = *Insight Pocket*
Guides
with Pull out Maps

Insight Compact Guides

Algarve
Amsterdam
Bahamas
Bali
Bangkok

Barbados
Barcelona
Beijing
Belgium
Berlin
Brittany
Brussels
Budapest
Burgundy
Copenhagen
Costa Brava
Costa Rica
Crete
Cyprus
Czech Republic
Denmark
Dominican Republic
Dublin
Egypt
Finland
Florence
Gran Canaria
Greece
Holland
Hong Kong
Ireland
Israel
Italian Lakes
Italian Riviera
Jamaica
Jerusalem
Lisbon
Madeira
Mallorca
Malta
Milan
Moscow
Munich
Normandy
Norway
Paris
Poland
Portugal
Prague
Provence
Rhodes
Rome
St Petersburg
Salzburg
Singapore
Switzerland
Sydney
Tenerife
Thailand

Turkey
Turkish Coast
Tuscany
UK regional titles:
  Bath & Surroundings
  Cambridge & East
Anglia
  Cornwall
  Cotswolds
  Devon & Exmoor
  Edinburgh
  Lake District
  London
  New Forest
  North York Moors
  Northumbria
  Oxford
  Peak District
  Scotland
  Scottish Highlands
  Shakespeare Country
  Snowdonia
  South Downs
  York
  Yorkshire Dales
USA regional titles:
  Boston
  Cape Cod
  Chicago
  Florida
  Florida Keys
  Hawaii: Maui
  Hawaii: Oahu
  Las Vegas
  Los Angeles
  Martha's Vineyard &
    Nantucket
  New York
  San Francisco
  Washington D.C.
Venice
Vienna
West of Ireland